Lessons from My Fiver-Year-Old Self

by

Charles Holt

© 2022 Charles Holt

No part of this book may be reproduced or transmitted in any form or by any means, electronic or mechanical, including photocopying, recording or by any information storage and retrieval system, without permission in writing from the author, except by a reviewer who wishes to quote brief passages in connection with a review written for inclusion in a magazine, newspaper or broadcast.

Printed in the United States of America Holt, Charles.

Lessons From My Five-Year-Old Self / Charles Holt
For more information visit www.theopenframesproject.org
Front cover image © digitalskillet
Cover design: Pip Abrigo
ISBN: 979-8-218-08253-6

Self-realization, Self-discovery, Self-emancipation, Freedom

Lessons from My Five-Year-Old Self

In Lessons from My Five-Year-Old Self, Charles Holt takes us on his life's journey of his self-discovery, self-actualization and growth through his experiences. Reading with an open heart, Charles's story teaches us love, forgiveness and a knowing that our soul directs our paths, if only we heed and trust it.
– *Ginger Campbell*
Principal, Snap Productions

LESSONS FROM MY FIVE YEAR OLD SELF

Personal Stories and Essays
on the Path to Self Discovery

By Charles Holt

Contents

Introduction

Lessons

Becoming I Am	1
In the Beginning	2
No Place like Lake Providence	3
Return to Your Soul	4
Where Did All These Rules Come From?	5
Go Back and Get It	6
I'd Like More of That, Please	7
Banzai	8
The Listener's Guide	9
You Can Run but You Can't Hide	10
Don't Get Stuck in The Mud	11
Surrender to The Truth of Your Heart	12
Provision Comes with The Vision	13
Manifested	14
Imagination is My Superpower	15
You Got This!	16
The Force of Internal Rage	17
In the Name of Jesus	18
Finding Freedom on Christopher Street	19

"If you would stop running around so much, and sit down and be still, then maybe the answer would come to you."

- Wilhelmina Holt

As a child, Granny was teaching me how to meditate even before I started to practice many years later. She was already ahead of the game. This was how she meditated. This was how she renewed her mind.

Introduction

I have experienced a glimpse of the essence of what I know to be my truest character and self, a few times. I am not talking about the obvious outer appearance that is seen through and by the natural senses, but rather a peering that can only be previewed through moments of insight. Some would call these spectacular showings "aha!" moments or bolts of realization. Many, like myself, confess to experiencing such flashes through verbal messages, vivid demonstrations, or striking illustrations. However, my first encounter was through a visual impression. It was a precise image, full of the design and detail of the face of my mortal recognition. But it was not the actual face that drew me. It was a feeling tone something I could not describe with words, that penetrated my Soul.

This snapshot of my original self called to surface the memory of what had already been etched into my DNA, even before I landed on the planet. For decades I scratched at its surface, searching for the nerve endings of what I felt when I first experienced it. After what seemed to be a lifetime of catching impulses, sources from all the paths that I had walked led me back to the screening room where I could remember the face of my authentic identity. Still intact, this identification revealed a view of a current reality, a unique compilation of my life and all that I had brought with me to that present moment. Scrolls, volumes, and an exposé of the good, the bad, and the awful unfolded in my mind.

The burden from a staggering combination of hopes and expectations stirred an impulse to dream beyond myself. Raising my head from watching the dust settle around my ankles was a saving grace. After a heady reflection of my past, I looked ahead to a vast field that I had not yet chartered. And though promising, these mountainous views on the horizon were intimidating. It was these moments that caused me to remember the first encounters of my youth, for they held within them a strong vibration of imagination to all that was possible.

Though not lengthy in time, this flash of insightful remembrance sustained itself long enough to activate within me a conscious journey back to my real self. So, what is the essence of life? It can be explained many ways, depending on the person. However, I believe there would be parallels and similarities that could be the connective tissue that would bind us all into a civil and moral knowing of what life is all about: Love, that is received and shared.

At five years old I granted myself the permission to have a thought, a voice, and even an opinion, despite the social and cultural codes. Though my mind was fresh in this new world, I came innately knowing that these things were my birthright. Life is no more than an idea waiting to be fully self-expressed. I was that idea. I was free to be my best, and free to do my best. I didn't have to compete with anybody else. My focus was on how much fun I could create, and not who I could blame for feeling stuck. What the present day could not manifest, within it held the possibilities of a thousand tomorrows. The best was always yet to come.

My dates with imagination became sacred courtships that yielded offspring of dreams come true. And after one dream was realized, I knew there was another great and grand idea waiting to come to me and through me. I believed in miracles because I witnessed them. I didn't know how they would appear; I just knew that they could. The luminous light of fireflies in summer's evening, the vibrant energy of dragonflies hovering on top of water, a drenching shower that quenched the scorching heat on an August afternoon, and a pile of leaves to run and jump into after Thanksgiving dinner. Miracles they were, and all very real to my young mind.

Introduction

When I think of life, I think of a place that we can call home—a physical space to reset and reflect; a grand concept and way of living; a civil arena where we can exist as unique individuals within a global community and universe, without the need to eradicate another living Soul. I think life calls us to moral and spiritual accountability—an understanding that talents, gifts, and skills may be different and carry a wide array of weight and favor, with the highest achievement resting upon our ability to share and demonstrate the gifts we have been given.

    I knew this to be true. I knew by the way it made me feel, and the emotions that I elicited. There was no shame to my game. I clung to a growing awareness that Life itself offers to each an abundance of creativity, prosperity, happiness, and peace. I saw this out pictured all around me. The demonstrations of my parents, grandparents, elders in my neighborhood, and teachers were quite influential. Yet, it was the abundance of nature and its language that sold me into knowing that what I was feeling was true. The trees and their vibrant colors, the bees and their ecstatic freedom, the birds and the roaming hills. Nature sang its harmonious, glorious melodies, and around me rang the music of life. All of it, broad, fluid, languid, expressive, creative, and procreative. I innately knew that my life was full and rich by what I saw through nature. Possibilities were everywhere, happening all the time. This was real to me; I felt the notion of this every morning I woke up. Ready for the day. Ready for the fun. Everything I needed was already provided.

    In addition to nature's message, my grandmother taught me that our stories matter. My parents taught me that I matter. My elders and ancestors taught me that our lives matter – all our lives. For without each possibility of life there would be less of its contagious force and grace. Life creates life. I know that life has always existed and shall never die.

All of this was made possible through the vast landscape of my imagination. Like my ancestors who rose from the shackles of slavery, I too understand that to be physically free is a necessary thing. But through their continued instruction and guide, I am persuaded that there is nothing compared to the emancipating of the entire being. To be free in one's mind is the ultimate liberation, and that freedom made imagination accessible. The hallmark of my life has been captured in the ability to stretch into the outer realms of what seems to be restricted by social rules, cultural coding, religious doctrine, and even forces unseen. However, the virtue of freedom that I know is up leveled, and high vibing. It has given me a channel to fully express who and what I am. In my challenges and times of greatest contrast, my imagination has saved my life, allowing me the opportunity to dive deeper into the flow of what I shall become.

Lesson 1

Becoming I Am

My parents had grown up nearly a rock's throw from one another. My father grew up with an older brother. The two of them were extremely close. You never would see one without the other. It was all about being frugal in their household. Though only two mouths to feed, my grandparents made sure that she squeezed as much out of a dollar as she possibly could. Grandpa, as his grandchildren called him, died when I was three years old. I didn't get to know him, but my mother insists he thought I had fallen from the clouds. "Your granddaddy loved you more than anything," she says.

    My mom, like my father, grew up in a time that held drastic and different conditions. She was born in 1929, on the heels of the Great Depression. I am sure that my mother's parents hunkered down to very basics to make ends meet for their seven children. Much of what my mother believes was cemented during one of the most economically challenging periods in American history—family was all that you had during those times. "And you learned to survive with all that you had," she adds.

    Whatever kind of work one could manage to get, you held on to it with your very life. For most, there weren't many options to choose from. There were no thoughts of trying to change jobs, occupations or vocations. Options were limited. "If you could get a job as a teacher, or if you were called to the ministry to preach, then you were in a better seat than some others," my mother reminisces. Being a preacher or a teacher were high standards and consistent pay back then. Due to layers of responsibilities within the family, there was no allowance for long searches in finding the "right" job. Supporting your family was first and foremost. You got what you could get, and you stayed with it. It's no wonder my parents held on to everything so tightly.

  Being a Christian was par for the course. Besides securing one's afterlife, Christianity was the foundation for everything. Growing up in a Christian home was mandatory and the ritual of being submerged under water became a key act of religious doctrine and one's conviction to their faith. Christianity was the religious structure that was seemingly above all others. At least that was what I was taught to believe. Religious rules were not the only grounds that had been set firmly into place. Guidelines surrounding family and education were also deeply tied to perpetuated beliefs that hold strong to roots of survival, even today. These standards were created in helping past generations in sustaining their existence. I understand it. It wasn't easy living in a society yet trying to find its traction on humanity and freedom. Yet, I wished my parents could've been more sensitive to the time when I came along? Why were they so set in their ways? I now understanding, but I came for a different type of experience.

Regardless of how old fashioned I thought my parents were while I was growing up, I clung to their teachings. It's what I knew to do. As I grew older, I obliged even when I felt that a particular judgment was going against what I knew to be true at my core. At the age of 22 doors began to close shut. I left a dream job of two years with IBM, only to be released a year later from another promising employer. The young lady, to whom I was engaged, decided the relationship we had fashioned would not work as a marriage. With the prospects of my living out the dream that I'd been taught to pursue, I realized that many things I'd been taught to seek to achieve did not belong to me. I was living out the wishes of others. Steeped in well wishing, the path that my parents and grandmother had steered me toward could only, at best, lead me to a path of discovering my unique, innate desires. Though I was disappointed at being terminated from Corporate America, and for the breakup with my fiancé, I was not close to being broken. In fact, each seemed to be weights lifted from my shoulders. I took a moment to reassess my situation before allowing the truth of what I had felt and known for many years to lead the way, with the guidance of the Universe.

My paradigm of thoughts and beliefs began a drastic shift. I started to become more confident in following what I now know to be my inner guide. Even in my years as a teenager and early adulthood, I felt that I had a unique path of my own design to follow. Today, I have fully embraced this knowing. I never would have been able to use the tools in finding my way to my path without my parents giving me a strong foundation of principals, and for the great contrast their way of living offered me. I am eternally grateful for coming to the planet through them, and what they shared with me once I arrived.

Blessed are my parents and ancestors for their fortitude to survive, thrive and achieve in the forward of evolution. I believe what they could not express due to lack of information and vocabulary, was made palpable through their demonstrations. Their mode of teaching served as a template of how to live a human life and understand the authentic self.

    I realized that there was much more to learn beyond my parents' guide, however. I knew I was here to fashion my own way to live this life. Through emotional pain, disappointment, misunderstanding, and seeming setbacks that I was here to fashion my own way to live this live … this path that I call my life. Flipping to the other side of the coin would mean great, grand, and glorious gains.

    It has taken decades to become conscious to this truth. By decoding from congealed, negative information, and weeding through beliefs that no longer serve me, I continue releasing myself from the paralyzing mercy of

Lesson 1 - Becoming I Am

thoughts and opinions of others. I am finally able to discern the thoughts that belong to me and the thoughts that do not. I am aware of the past that I had been thrust into. I now see, since learning how to unmask the myriad of disguises and protective coverings I, like my parents, donned for the sake of self-preservation and acceptance. Many of the beliefs that fostered the courage of my parents could only hold the space while I became conscious of the truth of myself. I understand that their greatest charge to me was that I learn to set sail on my own journey to freedom and self-realization, given the benevolent example they'd endured. Perhaps the lesson indicated through all their prayers and efforts was figuring out who I am by learning who I am not. Only through the security from trusting my own intuition and inner guidance would my destiny be sealed.

I have realized that some things I have chosen during my journey may not have been in full alignment with my highest good, but I will not beat myself up about that. I will, however, know that the pattern of my design is fully capable of reconstructing and restitching seemingly frayed fibers back into the original fabric of my being.

I am still carving my way back to my original portrait. This time I am conscious of the passageways, the intersections, and the bumps in the road. And although there are still bumps in the road, I allow the growing wisdom to speak to the situation, circumstance, and condition, knowing that deep inside of my being all is well. All things are flowering in a way that I can only describe as transcendent and magical.

Lesson 2

In the Beginning

My life was good on all fronts at five years of age. I was surrounded by love, especially from a grandmother who I adored. Both of my siblings were over a decade older than me, and I stayed with Granny until one of them or my parents would come to take me home.

"In 1868, a missionary by the name of Larry A. Thompson, declared the providence of God had led him to a particular field that was filled with brush and weeds," she'd begin. Granny was born in 1901 and she'd tell me stories about our community and its beginnings. Handed down, she would use her own spin in telling tales, assuming the voice of Rev. Thompson. "God has given me a vision, and right where I stand, I will build my church." He named it Lake Providence Missionary Baptist Church. "Where'd the 'lake' come from, Granny?" I asked. As the story goes, there used to be a flowing creek on the northern border of the community where new converts were baptized. This changed when a new church was erected in 1950 with a baptismal pool in it. The heavy stream still runs but has since been covered with trees by its banks.

My formative years were heavily influenced by what I heard and saw demonstrated while I stayed with her. I was enchanted and enthralled by my grandmother's stories. Granny was also a self-taught pianist. A treat she'd offer, along with one of her tall tales, was a song. Granny's voice wasn't that of a sweet songbird, but she sure could put the two together to make for a wonderful evening of performance in her "front room." I would sit on her sooty linoleum floor, inches between her bony knees and a rusty, potbelly stove. "Just open that big mouth of yours and repeat after me," she'd say.

Getting a restless five-year-old to sit on the floor for an extended period of time took some skill. I wasn't always willing to sit through Granny's music lessons, however she somehow always managed to pull me in to her meetings. Music and storytelling are the tandem that won my attention. They were inseparable, one always giving space to the other in a seamless way.

My grandmother set the stage for me to feel music. Songs became catalysts for me to recognize my emotions. Sensitive, I could relate to a song by the way my grandmother sang it. I noticed how it moved her, even to tears at times. From a raspy tone and altered pitch, there was something that came through the notes that she sang that struck the core of my being.

Growing up in a small rural community meant that I had to follow a long list of rules. Staying with my grandmother was no exception. I could manage to obey most of them, however there were some it seemed I couldn't

Lesson 2 - In the Beginning

reach at all. "Children are to be seen and not heard" was a staple of the Southern social tapestry, and a code that I always seemed to break. I couldn't quite find the place in me to shut up when meeting someone—especially for the first time. I was a natural communicator. However, verbal lashings served as adequate reminders that I was stepping across the line.

Behaviors that strayed from basic beliefs were discouraged and thrown from the center's governing structure by the spin of ostracism, social abandonment, and harsh judgment. After years of trying, I learned that I could not win at tempting to challenge a well-oiled system. But that's not to say I didn't try, and I did every chance I got.

Granny's house was sometimes filled with her gabbing friends. While in their presence, I would have to go to a corner in the room and pretend like I was doing schoolwork. Although I would try to persuade myself to stay focused on my studies, I couldn't help but listen in on the conversations. The voice inflections, the vocal tones, the embellishments, and the drama were all too enticing. Knowing that being curious could land me in hot water, I made myself as invisible as possible, and my movements subtle. I began by slowing turning my neck to I could peek over my shoulder. Although I didn't have a full-on view, the glance from the periphery did nothing but lure me in more. I wanted to see everything. With an ever so slight turn of my body, I could better position my head. I adjusted

my head so I could see more, and what I witnessed amazed me. The body language, the eye movement, the hand gestures, and the rolling of the neck - I was buzzing with sensory overload. If I could just get one more turn of my neck, I thought. But I got too comfortable, and too greedy. Then boom! "Now didn't I tell you to sit over there and keep your nose out of grown folks' business?"
My grandmother would stretch her voice across the room and cause everything inside of me to tremble. Quickly, out of my world of enchantment, I'd sober up, snap my body back into position, and put my face far into the creases of the book. After more than a few deep breaths, my heart rate would resume its normal state. Then my mind would recount what I had so desperately wanted to experience. What I had witnessed was worth a thousand memories.

With my full self-expression, there was no doubt in my mind that I was equipped to reveal the highest of principles and eternal qualities. Peace, abundance, happiness, joy, compassion, freedom, opulence, harmony, creative genius, wholeness, and love were all at my fingertips. And though I may have lacked the vocabulary in properly naming these virtues, I was familiar with the way they made me feel. I believed that we all innately possessed these inspired principles. And because we all have these within us, I knew we would be willing to fully experience them and share them with others. It was an ideal world that I lived in. Only later in life would I realize that the happy fantasy

Lesson 2 - In the Beginning

I had created for myself was in fact a valiant attempt at living my best life.

"Sometimes you may have to go by yourself,
but you will never walk alone."

- Charles Holt

Lesson 3

No Place like Lake Providence

The South was, and is still, a very interesting, magical place. So was the small community in which I grew up. Although Nashville was not classified as the Deep South like other cities as Montgomery or Mobile, Alabama, or Jackson, Mississippi, it still held the trappings of Dixie and the traditional Southern lifestyle. My community was the epitome of this down-home way of living. Notably, the way people talked. Most spoke in a slow, unrushed fashion. Words that were composed of one syllable were made to have two. For example, the word boy when properly pronounced has one syllable. In the South, it is pronounced as if you were pronouncing the word joey. So instead of saying boy we said boey with two syllables.

Although I lived eighteen years under my father's roof, there were many occasions that I furled my brow in trying to figure what he had said. "Bring me back a seu-mup from the store please," he once requested. "A what?" I asked him to repeat himself, trying to figure out what he'd said. He said it again, but I still didn't understand what he wanted. Luckily my mother was there to translate. "Bring him a 7-Up," she said. "Oh, a 7-Up." This made me giggle a little bit. Dad, or any of his colleagues in the community, did not pronounce the word seven as it was spelled. There was the s then the e and m; the m was pronounced like in the word hum. But there was no m in the spelling of seven.

    Typical Southerners didn't worry about too much. They took their time with things and loved a good 'ole cold drink every now and then. The translation for "cold drink" could be Coca-Cola, Pepsi, or the old favorite, RC Cola. Southerners usually were not in a rush. They moseyed to the bank, strolled to school, and sauntered to church. Summers in the south were special. All of nature revealed herself as we welcomed the season for shorts and t-shirts. And that time of year everything seemed to slow down even more. This could have been due to the weather; nature seemed to take on the same lilt as its cohabitants. The heat was stifling with a humidity index that could sometimes beat kids back into the house during summer recess. Afternoon thunderstorms often wafted in through a band of heavy, grey clouds. After a day of sweltering heat, you could always count on a late afternoon downpour of rain, that usually made the humidity even worse. Fall and winter made their entrances and escapes without too much wonder.

    The temperatures in October were crisp, a welcomed reprieve from a hot summer. Fall was my favorite season. I loved watching the leaves fall and gather on the ground. After Thanksgiving dinner, me and my cousins would go outside and pile them up into one big heap and run and jump into a colorful foliage the trees had willingly released. Winters weren't too harsh. The most extreme winter event would be an ice storm that would shut down the city for days. There was hardly ever an abundance of snow, but sometimes we'd get lucky with a blizzard that would dump a consideration amount snowfall to the ground. Besides the fact of not having to go to school, the snowstorm was plenty enough to make snow cream. My parents would put all the ingredients in, and I would sit and help churn it until it hardened. There was nothing like homemade ice cream from a fresh winter powder. It was cold, creamy, and quite a delicious treat. The ice cream made me happy, but the family effort warmed my heart. Chirping birds signaled that the end of the deep freeze was near. Slowly, the fresh blades of grass climbed the steep hills and high yards announcing the arrival of spring. By summer, lightning bugs, ladybugs, and honeybees were all in full flight. Dragon flies were my favorite. I used to sit and watch them skate across ponds filly their bellies with summer's nuisance, mosquitos. Honey suckles and all kinds of flowers were in full bloom, making everything smell delightful

  Summer was active and fun. Being out of school was a breath of fresh air for me, and my parents. Although dad liked to go rabbit hunting in the winter, he too welcomed the opportunity to hang out with his friends in the neighborhood. I remember times when my father would take me walking down the road. We lived on Goins Road, named after Reverend Willie Goins, who was one of the ministers at our church. Many of the streets in our neighborhood were named after celebrated residents—all of whom were stalwarts in the church and leaders in the community.

Our community was full of characters. Self-proclaimed griots like Mr. Frank Patton could always be found sitting on a tree stump, shaded by the branch of a full-grown oak tree near the edge of a busy street. "Come here son, I want to tell you a little something," he called. "You see this street right here? Well, it was once a dirt path. Today it's a major artery in the city running right through our little community." "Now ain't that something," he concluded? "Yes, sir it is," I responded. He was referring to Nolensville Road, a path once trod by the likes of cobblers, seamstresses, farmers, storeowners, lawyers, pastors, and prominent businessmen and women through the years, had become one of Nashville's major thoroughfares.

Mr. Frank's invitations were always with a willing smile and pleasant demeanor. He'd sit for hours talking about the history of the community. "I remember when this ... and I remember when that ..." he'd begin. Dad would often chime in with his own spin, affirming what Mr. Frank had already said. These stories were fascinating to my ears.

You couldn't have storytelling without music. The South is known for some of the most groundbreaking and celebrated music in the world. Gospel found its roots in the South; and country music wasn't the only thing permeating the airwaves in the heart of Dixie. Where I lived, kids would be in the streets dancing to Stevie Wonder, The Jackson Five, Earth Wind, and Fire, and The Isley Brothers in the wee hours of the morning. Old schoolers like my dad, would sit on the porch with their transistor radios, passing the steamy summer's day with Billie Holiday, Nat King Cole, and B.B. King.

Ray Charles was my father's favorite. Dad very seldom struck a chord of high-pitched laughter. It was sometimes hard to even get him to crack a smile at home. But when the music of Ray Charles played, he would sit up in his chair and begin smiling and tapping his feet. I even witnessed him snapping his fingers and bobbing his head to the beat. This type of conduct was unusual for my dad. To see him move about in such manner fascinated me. Though sudden, his outbursts were contagious, making me get up and begin to dance.

Dancing was part of my DNA. It didn't take much to cause me to bust a move. My father watched me get down to the beat. Seeing my father throw his emotional caution to the wind gave me all the reason to jump into my full expression. After the song would end, my dad would turn the volume of radio down to a whisper, and resume his regular, emotionless programming. His behavior left me confused. Perhaps, all that expression had caused my dad to feel as if he'd over stretched his emotional boundaries, needing a break. I, on the other hand, had a few more dance steps I wanted to try out. I sat patiently, trying to figure out if he was resting a spell before turning the music on again. Whether he decided to crank it up again, I was still grinning like a little Cheshire cat. Having the attention of my dad at that moment seemed to make up for the ways in which I felt shunned in the past. Being in his presence made life so much better, and it made me feel special.

As we got ready to leave Mr. Frank to the rest of his evening, my father saw a friend at the fruit and vegetable stand across the street and waved at him. Two noted families, the Pratts and the Maxwells, kept the people nourished. The community never lacked in sustainable food. What we now call organic, my parents and grandparents called "homegrown" when I was growing up. They didn't use pesticides or herbicides. They couldn't have afforded them either way.

As we continued our rounds through the neighborhood, the smell of food wafting from somebody's kitchen would catch our attention, and our appetite—aromas that made your mouth water and your bellies yearn. There were great cooks in our community, but hardly any could rival my mother. Fried chicken, macaroni and cheese, green beans, turnip greens (my favorite), creamed potatoes (sweet potatoes for Dad), and hot water cornbread was a favorite menu. A glass of lemonade or Southern iced tea (which always had loads of Domino's sugar) would seal the deal and any thirst you might have.

My mother, at ninety-three years of age, still loves the thought of cooking. Now, she can only reminisce of the days when she could stand in the kitchen for hours with her favorite recipes. Southern cooking with a unique, colorful home-style quality is the way I would describe Mom's dishes—the right flavor, the perfect seasoning, topped with her own special, made-from-scratch blend ... Oh, and not to forget that it was always prepared with Mom's love. Dad would pile his plate sky high. Within a matter of minutes, it would be gone. And in a fantastic finish, he'd wash it all down with a king size glass of water. Eating and dashing off to be with his friends was about the only thing that my father made haste of. In hindsight, I believe that his rush could have been left over from his days serving in the Army. It would take me a little longer to finish my meal, since I'd spend the first few minutes staring at Dad's heap, wondering how he was going to manage all that food in his fit, slender body.

There were no age limits when it came to honoring and respecting the older citizens. Making sure the elders of the community had basic needs like water and food was mandatory. In my neighborhood there were many houses that did not have indoor plumbing, including my grandmother's house. In the middle of their yards were water pumps and faucets. I was my grandmother's water boy, always making sure she had plenty to drink, especially in the summer, which could be quite warm in the South.

My grandmother, like other neighbors, had an outhouse. They were located a few yards from the dwelling for sanitary reasons. "Granny what happens if you have to get up in the middle of the night to use the bathroom?" I asked. "Well, most times you didn't have a choice, you'd just have to get up and make the trip outside at two o'clock in the morning," she said.
Though in our house we had running water with proper plumbing, my father and my mother grew up without it. There were nights I would awaken to my dad leaving to go to my grandmother's outhouse, the one he had grown up using. What a habit to have – pacing through the night to the loo to do "number two." I could only imagine how that could feel, in a dark, tiny, smelly toilet. I wondered how anybody could sit in this dark, scary place and be comfortable enough to complete their business? I would sometimes choose to use Granny's "bathroom" when I stayed with her, only if I had to do "number one." However, after a few trials, I decided I would hold everything until I got home.

In our community, to be of service was noble and expected, but one could also make a little money from doing chores. Mrs. Flora Maxwell was one of the preacher's wives, A lovely, yet stern woman, she also had a street named in her honor. Her husband owned houses and some land; he rented to many citizens in our little community.

His biggest asset was his food store. Not only was Maxwell's Produce Market a blessing to the Lake Providence community, but it also became one of the most sought-after markets in the city Nashville and surrounding areas. Mrs. Flora would often ask my grandmother if she'd like to come and skin onions on occasion. Since I stayed with Granny, I would go along and earn a few quarters to help with my summer treats. A good 'ole snow cone could be the best way to quench the heat from a hot summer day. Mrs. Flora would sometimes invite another friend named Edna Taylor. Mrs. Edna was the queen of skinning onions. She was a real short lady in stature and was one of the most beloved members of our community. She always wore a smile and glasses with thick convex lenses that made her eyes appear much larger than they were. I would sit next to Mrs. Edna in order to find out what her secret was to skinning so many onions in a sitting. I tried my best to keep up with her. She seemed to be as casual as Granny and Mrs. Flora, but at the end of the day, she would have skinned nearly twice as many onions as everybody else.

    Determined to top her efforts, I decided to forgo the ten-minute break, and while they were up stretching, I continued my race to the finish. I knew I had quite a bit more to skin just to catch up with Mrs. Edna. She had gotten off to a blazing start, nearly clearing three crates in a matter of what seemed like minutes. I was confident I'd be crowned winner for the day. "Times up," Mrs. Flora said. "It's time to count up what we've done." We would all sit in our chairs, cleaning ourselves and our clothes from all the onion skin, waiting for her to make her final tally. "Well, you did it again, Edna. Here's a little extra for you."

I looked at Mrs. Edna's heap of crates. No! There is no way she could have outshined me. I didn't even take a break. Insulted, I asked Mrs. Flora if she'd made an accurate count of mine. "I'm sure I did, baby. Let me count yours one more time, okay." I waited with bated breath, carefully watching as she recounted the bunches, and watching her work the last bit of sugar out of the piece of juicy fruit gum that she chewed on. Well, she was right. Mrs. Edna had barely squeezed by me. I couldn't believe it. "Because you did such a great job today, here's a little extra change for you, too." I guess Mrs. Flora could see the disbelief and disappointment in my eyes. I thanked her and headed back up the hill with my grandmother.

When we got to Granny's house, she had a surprise waiting. After washing my hands from all the dirt and onionskin, I hurried to Granny's secret "chamber." She kept some of her valued clothes in an old chifforobe dresser, along with her wallet and change purse. "I'm going to give you a little gift for your time and for being so smart today," she said. "Granny's proud of you. Here's two dollars." I was raking in the money; it was flowing to me double! This really was a special occasion, because Granny rarely gave me anything above a dollar. The only other times during the year she'd exceed that amount was for Christmas and my birthday. December 19 was a day to look forward to because she would combine the gifts and give me a whopping ten dollars—five for each celebration.

"It's not what you get;
it's what you take care of."

- Clarence N. Holt

These words were spoken by my father as a way of inspiring me to be thankful for what I had, as well as a reminder to be responsible.

Lesson 4

Return to Your Soul

I am convinced that my appearance onto the earth plane and the beginning of this human life was, at best, a thrust into the past. The action of the doctor pulling me from my mother's womb into this world was a motion of being midwifed and shoved into a construct fashioned by the lives of those who lived before me. Back in time I went. I had no idea that nearly everything I was being taught by my parents, grandparents, and elders were ways of living, beliefs, rules, expectations, conditions, and regulations that had been handpicked from a vine of century old life prescriptions. I am also aware they did the very best they could with what they had.

After nearly five generations, I showed up on the scene. I wasn't in competition with anybody or anything. I didn't allow what others said about me to keep me from my joy. What others thought about me wasn't important. The only worry I had was whether I'd make to base before being tagged in a game of hide and seek. Playing outside with friends was big fun. Feeling the wind on my face in a spontaneously foot race was a natural tonic. This fancy-free attitude continued even when I started attending grammar school. Like life at home, school soon became a course in imagination in the beginning. The access to happiness was held within whatever I dreamed I could become. Friendships were abundant. The love I felt while surrounded by people who accepted me made it all work. My greatest joy was having the freedom to be what and who I believed I could be at in given moment.

As I matured in age, things began to slowly change. Matriculation through school seemed to offer many benefits of education and relationships. But at the age of eight years old it seemed my senses opened to a different perception of life. Becoming self-conscious, I was pulled into the world of paranoia and the effects of what others thought of me. The broadcast of information at home, religious rules, and social codes could be overwhelming at times. The seemingly smallest things I witnessed in school started influencing my behavior and my actions. I began to experiment with competition and comparison. Strict school regulations on how I should conduct myself added to an existing list of cultural and social orders. Having to stand in a single file line aggravated me most. Snickering and whispering by my classmates caused a subtle feeling of confusion, forcing me to judge myself and others as well. Instead of eagerly running to catch the school bus in the morning, I poked a long digesting the uneasiness the day from the day before. I began casting myself in to reclusion, far away from my innate well spring of creative imagination and joy.

Beginning the Swim Up Stream

When you're true to your authentic self, you're enthusiastic about life and everything around you begins to activate at that vibration. When you try to do what others think is more appropriate, life begins to drain of its color and vibrancy. The energy stops flowing. That's when the pushing begins.

The harder I pushed, the louder the chants in my head. Be more of a good little southern boy. Be more of a good little southern Christian boy. Be more of a good little southern Christian black boy. When I was eight years old, I began pushing my way into a world unlike the one I had known. Never in my young life had I negotiated what I liked versus the opinion of what someone else deemed appropriate. I censured my clothing, the colors I chose, the foods I ate, the people I talked to, and most of all the way in which I controlled my emotions.

Peer pressure was a relentless bully. With all the kids in my neighborhood, most of which were boys, I wanted to be considered cool like everybody else. I loved gymnastics and I loved to dance. However, these talents didn't quite make to the list of what boys should do. The last thing I wanted was to be made fun of or be called names like "sissy." So, I thought to my self, I should play baseball! I like playing baseball too. But acceptance is what I wanted most, and the only way I thought to be accepted by everybody was to become what I thought everybody wanted me to be.

My parents were the only influence that could seemingly stop the momentum of my actions. However, I was determined in finding my way through different means and opportunities. My playing popular sports satisfied my desires of fitting in, while winning the support of everybody else, including my mother. It took a bit of nudging Mom, but she finally consented. And once I started, I played every sport I could. Baseball, track, and football began to fold over my love of dancing and tumbling. I let it happen willingly, because I wanted to acquiesce to what everyone else thought I should be. I found ways to make gymnastics work, even though it wasn't seen as a popular sport for boys. The fact that I could do back flips and ariels won the praise of the toughest guys in our neighborhood. I made the All-Star baseball every year. I shined on the track as a sprinter. And I was a gridiron superstar. I was happy, but I was hiding parts of my true self, and the pushing had only begun. My mind became fixed on thoughts on the approval of others. Am I cool enough? Am I masculine enough? Do they see me as one of them? Am I enough? The final question was never satisfied. "You must do something extra to be enough," my mind answered. "You must be somebody else to really be liked and to be impressive, Charles. So, create yourself anew." Everything about me began to shift. Not only could I hear it. I could feel it.

Lesson 5

Where Did All These Rules Come From?

My world of discovery was neither a welcome to a present reality nor an invitation to a future trajectory. Most of what my wonderful parents knew, believed, and practiced was taught to them by their parents—a staunch list of hand-me-downs that had withstood the test of time. I'd been cast into a net that was held secure by generations of doctrines, superstitions, convictions, traditions, and codes. I dare say that these beliefs were void of benefits; however, the volumes of strict boundaries, what-to-do's, what-not-to-do's, and a stage of characters who'd been playing these roles for years and positioned everywhere for reinforcement, caused my perception of life to become blurred and confusing at times. Nevertheless, I began trying to conform.

My parents grew up during tough times that helped in shaping them, and their beliefs. Like the institution of religion, my family held tight to cultural codes that were imperative to their livelihood and existence. I came to understand this thinking, and I applied it. I am not sure that I had much to say about my parents' philosophy growing up, but I know how it made me feel at times. The close bonds of family can lead to feelings of obligation. Though I felt like a different approach to a situation could have caused a better outcome, I chose my parents' way of thinking in resolving the matter. As a result, I had ongoing bouts with feeling the burden of coercion and being drafted into the past. I believe the older way of thinking that my parents endorsed had its place and time, and I know that parts serve as a structural frame of support as my life continues to unfold. But much of what seemed like the umbilical tie to my family connection had to be reconsidered. There was some that had to be severed.

Anytime you have family ties, you have emotional cords as well. My experience with the presence of an emotional cord was that it seemed to constrict any idea of stretching toward a dream, particularly a dream that was out of the box of what was considered normal. These rules even applied when choosing location to plant roots. According to the older generations, staying physically tied together as a clan was the only way for a family to subsist. My parents and their kin weren't the only ones who lived accordingly. The entire community in which I grew up sanctioned this belief. I, however, wasn't sold. It wasn't until after I left for college that I was able to put a finger on the meaning of this type of behavior, and why this type of mindset had survived for generations.

Being Black in the South drew an iron of difficulty. These rules and apprehensions that became cultural staples

Lesson 5 - Where Did All These Rules Come From?

to existence stemmed from generational hand me downs that were reinforced through a type of mental and emotional bondage that yet existed. And as much as I defended my freedom, I understood my parents' stance. It all lead back to survival.

Fears, Myths, and Legends, Oh My...

My dive into the history of Black people in the United States, particularly those from the South, highlighted some of the most sacred social enigmas held within the beloved race and culture I had been born. The beginning of my understanding regarding certain rituals started to become clearer. I began with the study of superstitions. Crossing black cats, umbrellas in the house, splitting poles, and breaking glass mirrors were just a few of the myths that I tried unraveling. The first time I accidentally let an umbrella up in the house, my mother nearly had a heart attack. "Boy, let that umbrella down. Don't you know you'll have seven years of bad luck?" My grandmother was terrified of black cats. "Don't go near little devil," she said. "How is a black cat a devil, Granny?" "They say they are linked to Satan," she responded. How Ridiculous! I never mentioned to her, but Black cats were a favorite of mine. She would have disowned me and kicked me out of her house. Though I did not find proper reasoning to why these myths were held so tightly, however, one factor that caused them to become legendary was the component of fear.

Fear and trepidation seemed to inform many decisions my parents made, my mother especially. My grandparents were a little less extreme, but not by much. I recall times my father would wince at my travel to parts of the city during certain times of the day. "You need to be over on this side of town before the sun goes down," he insisted. Lines of separation had been drawn in our city, and in most of the South. Blacks and whites were divided on every platform. Firm agreements had been established through a system of segregation. In certain places the arrangement was sophisticated enough in fostering a tacit agreement. Even when the laws of segregation were disbanded, the heavy dust of separation still covered streets and neighborhoods in cities all over the country. The South was buried in the thickest soot.

The permit in allowing the past to govern life in the present became an airtight practice. My parents and the generations before them learned how to survive through a type of fear—one that assumed top priority, and subsequently squelched the impulse to dream beyond that which they could only see in front of them. My father would often chime in. "You had to always look over your back. You didn't know who had their eyes on you." Fear was a life force of survival through the ages, and it was a staple in conduct while learning the skill of adaptation.
Learning the rules of past generations was a way of finding

one's footing in a complex, confusing, and sometimes cruel world. I observed strains of this social virus early in my youth. Adages ruled the day, forcing me into submission of an old fashioned saying. "Children are seen and not heard." This proverbial saying of the elders in my community, was used to inform children of their proper place. As soon as I was older and brave enough, I would ask my parents the meaning of such. Asking such a question was frowned upon and labeled as "back talk." The answers were usually "because I said so" or "don't ask me to explain anything to you. I'm grown, and you are a child." I didn't think their responses were sufficient. When I asked for a different answer, I would endure much harsher punishment for being, what they called, "disrespectful."

    I fought against this type of suppression tooth and nail. I came to the planet fully self-expressed, knowing that freedom in all aspects was my birthright. My definition of "freedom" was different from my parents'. Times had changed. Things had advanced. Society was different. After a certain age, I decided that I would not imitate my parents' thoughts or ways of survival. I had a voice, and I was going to make sure I was heard.

Strangled by a Mother's Love

    Being the baby of the family by over a decade made it difficult to get a protective mother to sign off on extracurricular activities ... Can I go to the skating rink after school? ... Can I go on a class trip to my third-grade teacher's farm to see the horses? ... Can I go swimming at the Boys Club? ... Can I ride my bike up and down the hill? ... Can I take karate lessons? ... Can I spend the night with friends this weekend? ... Can I go on the school's hiking trip next month?" My mother's initial answer to all the above was an emphatic "No, you cannot!" The reason was always around her projection of something awful happening to me: "You'll drown in the pool. ... You'll either get kicked in the head by the horse, or you will be thrown from it. ... You'll fall and break your arm rollerskating ... You'll get hit by a car while riding your bike..." It went on and on.

    I was as relentless, as she was cautious. I persisted in challenging her at every corner, not because I was intentionally rebellious, but because my freedom was being held captive. I came to the planet free. I am still an ambassador of this great principle. Freedom is a birthright, and I knew it to be so at a very early age.

    I am grateful for the care of my parents. Their brooding over me served a great purpose in my life. I don't think they knew how to stop their hovering, though. I was spinning around in a world that was focused on fulfilling the desires of others. What could I be to please my father? What peace could I bring to my dear mother? It seemed harder and harder to discern what was up and what was down. I found myself floating in a bubble of oppression, suppressing a part of the fiber of my being.

    This speaks directly to our feelings, because the first step in recognizing the freedom to grow and become more of who we are is to become aware of how we are pushing against the innate feelings within our emotional body. The spectrum of emotions couldn't have found residence in my Mind, because of the way I was taught and what I was conditioned to believe about them. "Keep them closed up" was the motto for dealing with the way I felt. By the time I'd reached junior high school, I had but all but abandoned the connection with my emotions and feeling tones. I became aggressive with other males. I remember picking a fight with a one of my teammates over a cup of Gatorade. I acquired a deep conviction to competition and winning. I began keeping a distance from my friends for no apparent reason. I was reclusive at home as well, closely monitoring my conversations. At 15 years old I declared, "I'm on my own." It was my "me against the world" phase in life. I kept quiet, but I held tight to it. This was my sacred oath, and I shared it with no one.

    I was growing older and at the peak of puberty. An increase in testosterone was evidence that my body was maturing and that I was changing. However, the core of who I was began to unravel – and I felt it. My relationship with my mother and grandmother shifted. I didn't spend as much time talking with either of them like I used to. The gap between my father and I widened, and I began to resent him. The essence of my younger version was being pushed back. When I felt the impulse to jump on my bike and pop wheelies down the street; when I wanted to run outside and bolster a handspring into a summersault; when friends called for me to join them at David's Drive-In, our favorite neighborhood package store, something in my mind restrained me from doing so. Growing into adolescence was a big change from childhood. There were physical as well as emotional changes. The spectrum of feeling tones ran the grid much more frequent. Instead of learning to manage what seemed to begin a heightening of emotions, I threw caution to the wind and pretended that they did not matter, nor did they exist. I did not like what I saw myself becoming. I was far from the happy kid that I once knew. I wanted to fit in. I didn't know why, and neither did I desire to figure it out. I just wanted to feel like I was part of the group.

Lesson 6

Go Back and Get It

Who I was at the core of my being and what I had been taught to believe about myself had clashed head on. Once started, the cycle of becoming someone who you were not meant to be will continue unabated until something inside wakes up and says, I don't give a damn what they think about me anymore! I am going to be me. I was joyful as a child, before I bought into what everyone else said should make me happy, and I can be happy like that again. I may have to physically uproot from where I am. I may have to strike out on my own to find that feeling again. I may have to dig deeper than ever before, and peel back all the layers. But I know it's there, because I've felt it before, and I can feel it again.

    I felt a particular way when I went against my authentic grain. Acknowledging when I'd crossed these lines marked the beginning of reverence for my own emotional wiring. The impulse to leap out further resided in a broader spectrum of my being, a place where I could activate a greater part of myself. I had to go beyond personality and how I had been shaped by society, and the beliefs of the people around me. I was being called to reconnect with my emotional grounding, the key to my conscious unfolding good. The power in knowing this gave me the ability to start sketching the life I wanted to live. Facing my emotions with honesty wasn't easy in the beginning. I avoided and dismissed lots of things and thoughts that were deemed negative. However, some things I could not sidestep. But finding my flow became less about detouring difficult situations, and more about locating the feeling tone where I thrived and flourished. A big part of getting to that place was channeling my five-year-old self.

On July 6, 1996, I left my life in the South, which was all I'd ever known. With $400 in my pocket and a conviction that something was leading me down this unfamiliar road, I headed off to a new life in New York City. Although I didn't have a clue what to expect, I was certain that something greater than anything I'd ever witnessed or experienced awaited me. What I didn't realize was that I was about to embark on an adventure so profound that it would reshape my entire view of reality, and the spiritual and emotional cords that would soon be revealed.

Within days of arriving, I was already hot on the trail to my first job. I woke up at 7:30 a.m. to make an audition for the Broadway musical Rent. When I got downtown at 9:30 there was already a line of people wrapped around the entire block. I took my place at the end of the line.

For the next ten hours, I inched my way to those coveted studio doors, anxiously waiting for my turn to sing. Many audition veterans had brought books, homework, and music to help pass the time. I spent my time people watching. Enchanted by the whole scene, I found myself getting caught up in just how different everything seemed. I had an opportunity to see why New York City was called the melting pot of the world. No two people looked or sounded the same. I heard at least five different languages in the twenty-minute subway ride to the audition. People paced in overdrive. Never in my life had I seen people in such a rush to get somewhere.

Eventually, the sun began to disappear. Buildings began casting shadows, and I suddenly realized it was already 7:30 in the evening. I was within ten feet of the doors to audition, and I thought, wow, I finally made it. I am getting ready to have my first audition in New York City! I began my ritual of warming up my voice and taking deep breaths to stem nervousness. My legs were numb from standing all day, so I began running in place in order to wake up.

The door to the studio opened and I felt my body tense in anticipation. However, instead of inviting the next group of ten to come upstairs to sing, the audition monitor announced with a strong New York accent, "At this time we're not seeing anybody else. Please leave your headshot and resume in the box. If we like you, we'll call you. Thank you for your time and patience. Good night."

Dejected, I chose to walk through the Theatre District instead of taking the subway home. As disappointed as I was, the spectacle of Broadway and all its players was amazing. I began to picture the city as a giant fun house decorated with flashing lights, grand marquees, and fingers of fame all pointing at me through reflective mirrors. At the bottom of its doors were the words 'Enter At Your Own Risk' written in small characters.

    I stopped at a newsstand and picked up a copy of the week's Backstage, which many considered to be the stage actors' bible in New York. I saw an audition call for singers for the national touring production of Jesus Christ Superstar. Instantly I decided that I would attend. Before making it back to the apartment where I stayed, I decided to course through Colony Records to see if I could find a copy of the show's recordings. Colony was a premiere establishment located in Midtown Manhattan. Known for its extensive collection of music, everyone from Broadway actors, musicians, and music enthusiasts crowded the store's narrow aisles searching for popular scores and soundtracks. After purchasing a couple of different pieces of sheet music and CDs, I headed home with a renewed energy and excitement.

    The day of the audition for Jesus Christ Superstar had finally arrived, and I was beyond nervous. The closer the time came for me to leave for the audition, the more I thought about not going. Auditions made me feel intimidated. The fact that I didn't have formal theatrical training,

Lesson 6 - Go Back and Get It

like most of my peers, played the largest role in my lack of confidence. To a newcomer, auditions in New York were like walking into a circus filled with contortionists. There were people stretching parts of the body in impossible directions that resembled a pretzel. The halls to audition studios were filled with eccentrics at every corner. The restrooms were tuning chambers; never in my life had I heard such a symphony of chaos. I used every excuse I could think of, and the chatter that was trying to dissuade me nearly won. Then I had a sudden vision that woke me up. It was me on stage with Ted Neely, the original Jesus, and Carl Anderson, the original Judas, singing to sold-out audiences and screaming fans from around the world. Yet again, that five-year-old spirit had come to resurrect my confidence. Not without my bag of talents, I unabashedly jumped into deep waters, once again. My saving grace rested in knowing that as soon as I sung my first note, the quivering in my body would somehow align with the melody of the song, and fear would soon dissolve.

"How could I pass up this opportunity? Am I out of my mind," I thought? That did it. I flew out the door and headed downtown striding through the streets like a man on a mission.

When I arrived, I was thankful to see the line to audition for Jesus Christ Superstar was not wrapped around the entire block—only halfway. I was one of the last people in line, but the wait ended up being far less than half a

Lessons From My Five-Year-Old Self

day. As I entered the room, I went straight to the accompanist and handed him the sheet music to the title track of Aladdin, the song I prepared to sing. But at the last minute I asked his advice on singing something other than that. He suggested that I sing an anthem. Anthems were cool. My grandmother used to teach me anthems along with hymns and spirituals. I chose "America, The Beautiful" and then proceeded to audition. The accompanist played the intro, signaling me to begin singing. I took a deep breath and, out of complete terror, forgot the words to the song. I could see Mr. Rabin give me an encouraging nod, while playing the intro once again. As it neared the time for me to begin singing I my grandmother's voice in my head. "Just open that big mouth of yours and let the words come out." This was undoubtedly Granny's words, the same ones she used to get me to follow along with her in her house. She had passed the year before my move to New York City, but she was still present, cheering me on.

    When I finished, the entire auditioning panel leapt to their feet and applauded. Wow, they must have really liked my performance, I thought. I later found out that standing ovations were almost unheard of, and to rate one at a theatrical audition was quite extraordinary. After three rigorous days of callbacks the production team narrowed the field down to twelve—only six actors would be cast.

    The show's producer made a rare gesture of flying in to conduct the final callback. At the end of the day, the

Lesson 6 - Go Back and Get It

twelve of us left the studio and nervously waited in the holding area while the production team decided which six would be chosen to tour. The wait seemed like an eternity. I could hear my mother's overly protective voice and my father's disapproving voice both fighting for space inside my head to see which one would get the privilege of telling me how crazy I was. I felt the heavy weight of that bickering and, for a split second, sank into muddy dejection. But those words could only discourage my efforts for so long. I began to see them for what they were: powerless ghosts of the past. At that moment I realized I had stepped beyond my comfort zone. For that, I was proud.

The moment had come. I had to concentrate in order to breath as the names of the chosen actors were read aloud: "Danielle, please stay. Eddie, please stay, Seth, please stay, Charles Holt, please stay." I asked the person next to me, "Did he say, 'Charles Holt please stay?'" I couldn't believe it. In a state of happy hysteria, I immediately began calling family and friends to tell them the great news. I'd only been in New York for a month, and I'd already landed a national tour. I was initially cast as one of the twelve disciples, and several times I had the opportunity to play one of the principal roles. My character, Simon Zealots, had one of the hottest songs in the show. Each night of performance, I lost myself in the music, surrendering to the synergistic energy between audience and cast. I jumped around the stage hitting high notes, low notes, and everything in between. This experience brought back memories of that five-year-old dancing in our living room for my parents' friends as the "guest entertainment." The only difference was that everybody wanted to hear more, and nobody was there to tell me to go to my room. It made me realize that although my parents didn't understand the path I'd chosen, and how performing made me feel, this time I couldn't keep quiet about it. I finally understood performing was what my life was about, and I knew there was much more to come.

Lesson 7

I'd Like More of That, Please

January 1997

After touring Jesus Christ Superstar for six months on a giant sleeper bus, we returned to the east coast for our last performances at the Merriam Theatre in Philadelphia. Like all endings, the final performances were filled with high emotion. During the finale, fans rushed down the aisles to the lip of the stage with flowers, blowing kisses, and holding banners saying: "We love you, JC Superstar! Please don't go!" Of course, there were plenty of tears and hard cries as we made our final bows. After the cast and crew said our final good-byes, we all crowded into a room where the producers were throwing a farewell party. Between all the moments on the dance floor and the food and drinks, cast members found a still corner to reminisce about the past six months and what our plans were going forward. I knew I would be returning to New York, so during the run of the show in Philadelphia, I spent a few days traveling back and forth on the Amtrak train in order to find an apartment. Still emotionally charged and feeling like I was floating on a cloud, I gathered my luggage and book bag and headed out the door to catch the last train headed back to my new digs in the 'Big Apple'.

As I was leaving, Carl Anderson called me to him. Carl was the glue to our tight knit cast. He treated me like his little brother during the entire tour. "If there is anything you need, let me know. I'm always here to help you." Carl became a mentor to me. I used to stand in the wings and watch him perform. Him singing 'Heaven on Their Minds' was spell binding. Incredible! As a novice of the stage, I was always looking and listening for performances that moved me to the core. A rendition of a song being sung that transported me into an ethereal state – something far beyond the normal. Carl's performances did that for me. I would say to myself, "I want to be like him. I want to sing just like Carl Anderson." It was an honor being chosen as one of two understudies to Carl's character, 'Judas'. Though I never got the opportunity to go on for the role, Carl's command while singing became etched in my mind. I never turned down the chance to take heed to Carl's advice. "Charles, I need you to meet Peter Wise." "Peter, you need to hear Charles Holt sing," Carl explains to me that Peter Wise is the casting director for the hit show, Smokey Joe's Café, currently playing the Virginia Theatre on Broadway. Peter Wise mentions that he would be holding auditions for the Broadway and touring companies in February. He graciously extended an invitation for me to audition. "Thank you, Mr. Wise! See you in a month." I went back to New York and nestled into my new, Harlem apartment.

February 1997

I arrived half an hour before my call time at the Virginia Theatre, current named the August Wilson Theatre. There were hundreds of young men standing outside, waiting for their moment to audition. After I checked in with the monitor, I too returned to the street in search of a corner to shield myself from the wind and, most importantly, tune my vocal cords. Consistent with the climate in New York City during this time of the year, the weather was brutally cold. As people finished with their audition, space became available in the costume department, located downstairs of the main stage. For those of us who'd been waiting outside, warming up downstairs was a welcomed reprieve. "Charles Holt", the monitor called. I was among twenty-three other young men, staggered across the stage – all waiting for our moment to shine. "Charles, you will stand here." The monitor was precise, getting people in and out rather quickly. "When we call your name, you will give the accompanist your sheet music and proceed with 32 bars of your chosen song," he added. After three days of singing and dancing, the creative team whittled an initial swarm of actors down to a handful of prospects. The last day was a final glance for the creative team who were all sparsely seated around the theatre. They would be choosing our fate, giving us all one last chance to give the best performance of our careers. Still 'green'; not having been in the industry long enough to recognize important hints and clues, I exited the stage door and hoped for the best. On my way out, the monitor paused me at the door. "They really like you," he said. "Oh, Thank you," I responded. What a nice gesture, I thought, reading nothing more into than what he'd said. I was too busy replaying my performance in my head.

Wired from the audition, I decided to pump my nervous energy into the weight room. The gym I attended was close by, so I paced two streets over, picking my way through the entire audition like a fine-tooth comb. I thought a few robust rounds of bench press and squats would ease my mind, but I could not concentrate on anything other than notes and dance steps. My racing mind was getting the best of me. After about thirty minutes, I decided to forgo the last set of my leg workout.

It was time to focus on something else: food. Between the audition and the gym, I had worked up an appetite. West 52nd Street is in the heart of Midtown Manhattan, everything is at your fingertips, including some of the best delis and food shops. "I feel like having a salad with some chicken," I thought. As I stood in line to place my order, my phone rang. "Hi, Charles, this is the General Manager at the production company for Smokey Joe's Café. I would like to offer you the role in the First National Tour." I was

Lesson 7 - I'd Like More of That, Please

floored. "Hello. Hello, Mr. Holt, are you still there," she asked? Meanwhile, it's my turn in line to place my order. "Yes, I'm still here," I answered. "Would you like to accept the offer, Mr. Holt?" "Absolutely," I screamed! Everybody in the deli is startled, trying to weigh their thoughts about my mental health. After picking up my salad, I raced over to the office to sign the contract. "The cast has been touring since August, so you'll be joining them. Tomorrow you'll go downtown to be fitted for your costumes. Monday morning we'll send a car to pick you up and take you to the airport. You'll be flown out to meet the company as they start their run at the Murat Theatre in Indianapolis. Once you arrive, the company manager will have someone transport you from the airport to the hotel where you will be staying. The company manager will make sure you have everything you need once you get there." My head was spinning like a top. "Any questions," she asked? "No," I hastily remarked. I could hardly breathe, let alone generate anything in my head in the form of a question. Given that I only had three days before leaving, I repacked the two suitcases from the Jesus Christ Superstar tour. I didn't know how long this tour would last, but before leaving, I agreed to pay my monthly rent to secure a place to live whenever I returned.

Being part of the cast of Smokey Joe's Café was a dream come true. Who would have imagined that my meeting Adrian Bailey in 1994, while he was in a production of The Boys from Syracuse at the Alliance Theatre, would give me impulse in moving to New York City two years later? After hearing me sing at an open mic event, he gave me some homework. "I want you to do yourself a favor. When it's available, go and get the soundtrack to Smokey Joe's Café. It's a new Broadway show that I will be part of. I believe your voice would sound great singing this music," he said. He was right. I loved the music, and I learned every song on the cast album. In the summer of 1996, I moved to New York and the show that I dreamed of being a part of became a reality for me. I had a lucid imagination, and it didn't hurt that I got a job as an usher at the theatre so I could put what I'd been listening into action. But I never would have dreamt that my life would unfold quite like this.

Like the imagination of my five-year-old self, I was ready to manifest new, bigger things. Things happened so quickly with my career as a performer that I couldn't put a pulse on what I was feeling. Flying by the seat of my pants wasn't such a bad thrill at all. My life, in my eyes, was rich and luxurious. After boarding planes and jet setting around the country, it seemed at every corner there was yet another grand adventure. A month after finishing the national tour, the cast boarded the plane to Japan for a month. This was my first trip out of North America. Though I had not previously visualized myself performing in another country, I'd always wanted to share my talent with the world. Meet-

Lesson 7 - I'd Like More of That, Please

ing people from different places and being immerse in a foreign culture gave me a feeling of oneness. I believe me knowing as a young boy that humanity was only separated by distance led me to this highpoint in my budding career.

After a thirteen-month run with Smokey Joe's Café, I got an opportunity to travel Europe, starring as Rocky in the Rocky Horror Picture Show, the first African American to have such a rare treat. Most of the touring cities were in Germany; however, we managed several stops in the Netherlands, Austria, Italy, and Switzerland. It was during the winter months and our time exploring places was shortened by freezing temperatures and a tight schedule from one city to the next.

Shortly after returning to New York from the tour in Europe, a friend put me in touch with a very prominent Broadway director. He was casting a New York City workshop of a new musical called Souls.com. Known for his innovative genius in both theatre and film, he had worked with some of my favorite actors, including Carl Anderson, in earlier productions of Broadway hit shows Hair and Jesus Christ Superstar. He was casting for a new musical portraying four music icons from that era – Janis Joplin, Jimi Hendrix, John Lennon, and Marvin Gaye. He had already chosen actors to play the three former roles and was looking for an actor to play Marvin Gaye to complete the list. "Have a seat and we'll get started here in just a minute," he said.

Lessons From My Five-Year-Old Self

The director's loft apartment in Union Square was where the auditions were being held. I walked off the elevator, directly into the eleventh-floor studio space. "Mr. Holt, are you ready to sing for us," he asked? I rushed to get my sheet music. "You won't be needing that. "I just want to hear what you sound like." An accomplished musician, he began tinkling some music from Gaye's most popular songs. "What are you going to sing for us?" "Let's do a little bit of my favorite," I suggested. I start singing "What's Going On." He begins to play along. Mid way through the song, he looks up at me and gives a quick nod of the head. He then looks at the creators of the show, standing directly to his right. They give what looks to be a concurring gesture. "Well, looks like we've found our Marvin Gaye," he said.

We began rehearsals and after a successful summer of run-throughs, in September, there were a few performances by invitation, hoping that the production would pique the interest and the wallets of a willing producers. We'd heard very little word about the next phase of Souls.com, and things were beginning to pick-up in the city now that most of the industry was returning from summer recess and vacation.

In mid-October, I received a call from the casting director for Disney's Lion King. He was interested in seeing me for a replacement role in the Broadway company. Though it was a four-month contract, Lion King was at the

Lesson 7 - I'd Like More of That, Please

top of my wish list. After opening in 1997, the show had played to sold out crowds every night. A blockbuster hit for sure with the likes of it not seen before on the stage. I dreamed to be part of something this special. The audition was held in the afternoon at Chelsea Studios, located a few blocks from the Theatre District. I arrived in a panic, thinking I was late. The lobby was empty; there was no monitor on the floor for direction. I followed the voice I heard down the hall. "Down here." I saw a head peek around the corner. When I got there, I saw three guys sitting in a row next to one another. About that time a man came out of the room. "You all can follow me, please," he said. In the room was Mark Brandon, the casting director, a man at the piano, and a younger gentleman with dreadlocks in the middle of the studio. I guessed that the latter would be instructing us through the dance portion of the audition. Mark Brandon instructed us of how things would progress. "We will be deciding today. One of you gentlemen will be getting a call this evening to be offered the role," he added. I don't know why auditioning for a role with only three other actors terrified me so much. What a drastic shift in numbers. I had just started expecting calls with lines out the door, given that both Jesus Christ Superstar and Smokey Joe's Café had been the that extreme. I was last to be called in to sing. The man at the piano was standing instead of sitting, which I thought was unusual. "Hi, my name is Joseph Church." As the show's music director,

I anticipated a more involved vocal tryout. "We're only interested in one thing for this audition, Charles. We want to know if you can hit a high C." He plucks the note out on the piano. Mr. Church proceeded with a series of scales on the piano. Afterwards, we are instructed to go back out of the room until we are asked to return for the dance part. The four of us were escorted back into the room to learn the choreography. After we'd moved through the choreography, the audition was complete. Within thirty minutes we are all released. "Thank you for coming in. We wish you all the best."

    I walked around the city with my phone practically glued to my ear. As the evening wore on, I began feeling less confident that I would be the one to receive the call. As 10:30 approached, I decided that I had not been chosen. With hope that one of my friends had been selected for the role, I dialed his number. As his phone rang, the voicemail alert flashed on my phone. I immediately hung up and retrieved my message. "Charles Holt. Charles Holt, this is Mark Brandon. Where are you? I've been trying to contact you all day. Get in touch as soon as you get this message." I called immediately. "Congratulations! We finally got you one. Welcome to The Lion King, Charles!" Almost speechless, I accepted the offer and got my instructions for costume fittings for the following week.

    As I played the conversation over and over in my head, one sentence stuck out more than any of the others.

Lesson 7 - I'd Like More of That, Please

Mark stated, "We finally got you one." Mark had been a supporter of my work for months, helping me get auditions for other shows he was casting. Lion King was my first Broadway show. It is what I moved to New York to accomplish. My dream of being on the grandest stage in the world had come true. I know it takes talent to book a job, but there is nothing like having the people who make the decisions on your side, rooting you on.

The following week I began rehearsals. My Broadway debut was December 17, two months after my initial rehearsal, and two days before my birthday. My opening night in Lion King changed my life, giving great testament to my five-year-old self who kept imagining the best life he could live, knowing that one day his dreams would manifest in an unimaginable way.

There aren't words to explain what it was like walking down the aisles in the back leg of our elephant Bertha – the back, right leg to be exact. The costumes, the lights, the music, and the energy were unmatched. With an initial contract of four months, I ended up being a part of the Lion King cast four years and eight months. Again, far beyond anything I'd ever
expected.

"We love you and are always praying for you."

- Mrs. Martha Patton
church Mother and neighbor

One first Sunday morning church service, during the ritual of The Right Hand of Fellowship, Mrs. Martha's words penetrated my young mind and connected to my heart. I knew she meant what she said, and I never forgot it.

Lesson 8

Banzai

Long before its original opening night, Lion King had come under strong criticism from some of the industry's most assuring opinions. It only took the world to experience the cast of Lion King's mesmerizing 1998 Tony performance to be convinced of its compelling magic and brilliance—a magic that perhaps had never been cast on a performance stage before. Hence, the story of a coming-of-age lion cub began its reign as one of theatre's most beloved and spectacular productions in history. In December 1999, I joined the cast. By this time, Disney's Broadway hit had assumed a stride and prowess of immeasurable success. Barely passing the two-year mark, thousands waited in line to draw tickets to the sold-out performance. The New Amsterdam Theatre, which had been vacant for years, was now residence to the king of Broadway.

My favorite character in the show was Banzai, one of the notorious, nasty trio of hyenas. It was a role that I'd coveted ever since joining the cast. With all The Lion King characters, I had been drawn to a minion of the key nemesis to Simba's ascension to the top of Pride Rock. Of course, Scar, Mufasa's brother and Simba's uncle was titled as the supreme culprit; however, he could not have

Lessons From My Five-Year-Old Self

crafted his devious plan without the help of his faithful followers: Banzai, Shenzi, and Ed. These three appeased Scar's every command in order to eventually settle for a morsel of food that always left them literally begging for more. This fancy of playing characters that served in the catapult of the hero's pride had always seemed to garner my attention. Though I had played the role several times as understudy during my first year in the show, I had dreamed of taking over the principal role someday. Once I found out the role was ready to be recast, without patience I made the management and creative team aware of my interest. I had gone through what I thought to be the proper channels to make sure that my request for consideration would be taken into full account. However, I did not get the role. When the new Banzai was announced, I was devastated. I knew that role better than anybody. Why was I overlooked again?

    The day to welcome the new cast member who would be taking over the role arrived. I stormed into the theatre, carrying with me a sting of bitterness and a chip on my shoulder. Still steaming over the fact that my performances in the show had seeming left me hungering for the elevation from ensemble to principal, I sank in my seat as his name was announced. "Please let us welcome Drew to the Lion King family." A thunderous applause ensued.

    After not being cast in the role, I dreaded going to the theatre, knowing I would have to endure the haunting

Lesson 8 - Banzai

of an unfulfilled dream for at least another year. It felt like someone was driving nails into my heart. My resentment began to overtake my attitude, and my actions shifted from support into being weighted in the opposite direction. Instead of welcoming the new Banzai, I acted as if I had taken on the role of resident director. I thought, "I'll decide if he is fit to play the character." I watched every move this guy made in rehearsal, looking for every misstep that countered the performance of what I felt I had mastered. I began searching for mistakes and places in which he had not quite become proficient in his short learning. "That was a wrong character choice. Banzai would never respond that way ... No, stupid, the right foot first, not the left," I mumbled to myself. My objections to his attempts were endless. I took pleasure in finding ways to criticize his efforts, and I was soon voicing my disapproval in cast meetings with the creative team by challenging his explanations to character choices. This was bold of me given that the show's director, along with those who'd chosen to hire him, were present. I didn't care. I wanted to make sure my commentary was being heard, and that Drew felt the sting of my irritation.

    After he had settled into the role, I continued to offer verbally offensive jabs. One Saturday evening I found myself pacing down the stairs from my dressing room to the stage. I knew he would be there stretching before the show. I purposely took my place some feet behind him to prepare as well, ready to conjure up a snide, foul comment to throw at him.

This kind of behavior was directly opposite of how I governed competition in my early youth. In fact, I hardly regarded competition as somebody being against me or me them. My dreams were much more important than giving my energy trying to ward off someone else's success. Choosing to demean another is a behavior eventually poisons any dream and endeavor, and I felt the heavy weight of my deeds upon me. Allowing a deeply disappointed part of myself to be the star of my show was causing everything to dim inside me.

As I carefully watched him limber up, a voice spoke to me: "Charles, you are wrong. You are out of alignment with who you are. You're treating him way beyond the scope of respect, and you have crossed every line. You must apologize." Apologize? Before I could dispute again, I heard the command, "Do it now!" I immediately recognized this voice. It. It was speaking from the inner most part of my being. This was a wake-up call that had come to remind me of my own truth and character, breaking the spell of my vengeful intention.

Heeding the voice of my inner knowing, nervously I began to walk towards him and stepped in full view. "Drew, I have something I'd like to say to you." By this time, he seemed to have learned to shun my very existence, and rightfully so. However, he did respond, "What is it you have to say to me, Charles?" Like an anxious child, I took a deep breath. "I apologize. I apologize for all the things I have said and done to you. I was wrong, Drew, and out of line for treating you the way that I have. Please forgive me." He looked at me, and then lowered his head in a contemplative manner. Feeling awkward and not knowing what else to say, I retreated to my dressing room. As I began to walk away, I heard him respond. "Hey, man. I forgive you. We're good," he added. Stunned, I stopped in my tracks. I didn't know what to say. I knew that I wanted to make it right and not make it seem that my gesture was a passing fancy, or something I wanted to get off my chest. I was sincere and genuine in my offer. I asked if we could find time to talk further after the show. He agreed.

"Why were you so rude to me?" he asked. "You seemed to hate me from the minute I walked through the door." As he paused, I put my head down and began to replay all my foul behavior in my mind. Remorseful for my insensitive and verbally assaulting deeds I became emotionally charged, on the verge of tears. All I could think about was how I had purposefully created an environment for someone to feel so uncomfortable around me. Where had I begun to resolve to anger towards others? When had competition caused me to be hateful towards someone else? I was far from this behavior and consciousness as a child. In fact, I was the exact opposite. However, my journey of detaching from a less competitive and more sensitive child to the aggression of rivalry and thick-skinned sensibility had caused an eventual turn in behavior. I rapidly scanned through my life, remembering experiences where I had used verbal bullying in attempts of making others feel inferior and myself superior as an athlete. Most of my actions were due to my neglect of lingering wounds from emotional pain. In this case, I allowed jealousy, envy, malaise to hijack my character. Drew wasn't the first person to encounter my wrath, but my experience with him had been my most extreme demonstration as an adult. I couldn't remember a time where I had worked so hard against someone else's success. My actions were a clear sign of how unhappy and divorced from emotions I had become.

    As we continued to talk, he asked, "Who did you think I was when you first met me? We knew nothing about one another prior to my coming to the show." Embarrassed, I once again lowered my head, trying to call on courage to help me respond. I said, "The moment I saw you I immediately noticed the self-confidence you carried. You didn't put it on. You wore it as if it had always belonged to you. It wasn't part of your personality. You were comfortable with it, and you never allowed anything said against you to take it away." His demonstration of power was intimidating to me. Drew's self-confidence revealed a strength I'd searched to find in myself for years. "But Charles you are the epitome of strength and courage, brother. Look at you." His kind words made me feel good, but I still felt a little odd hearing someone speak to my influence in such a way. All my life it seems as if everyone else could see these characteristics of myself, except for me. "I feel that I have chased these qualities my entire life. And though I have attained many accolades, achievements, and awards, claiming my own approval has seemingly escaped my grasp every time. But you, Drew—you have it. It is all over you. The way you talk, your posture, the way you respond to others, and the way that you share your artistic gifts and talents."

Both convinced the dialogue that we'd engaged in was far from roles in a show, our conversations continued. The more we talked, the more genuine, and transparent I was able to be. We would sit for hours and talk about our lives, our stories, our dreams, our failures, and our triumphs. "You know, Charles, you have always had power and courage. You carry it well. But if you are not aware of that, then what you see in others will never show as a reflection of your own possession of it. It will continue to elude and frighten you if you never come to the realization that you own it as well. Once you come to understand this, then what you recognize in others will no longer be intimidating or threatening, but rather serve as affirmation of who you are as well. That is a secure platform for self-validation."

Drew's words were self-confirming. In quick reflection, I realized I had persevered trying to find the next big thing—the thing I thought would make me happy and give me full satisfaction. But by the time I had a few rounds with success on the Broadway stage, television, and the silver screen, I'd reached a point where nothing I attained was enough. The thrill of the victory became short lived. My level of gratitude was growing stale. My appreciation for the gift of my craft got lost in the lights and applause. And round after round, within a short period of time I was back to coveting the next thrill. This was my way of getting praise from others, which in turn made me feel good about myself. As a result, my life became all about doing and appeasing. And it was in trying to do more than needed that my life seemed to become undone.

    I don't believe praise from others is something that we should not expect or seek to experience. However, for me, the relentless call for attention and adoration became my nemesis. Like a drug, my unyielding plea for praise soon made me numb to my own self-realization. Self-discovery and self-realization are two vital states of awareness that help in carving paths to self-fulfillment and self-worth.

    As Drew demonstrated, there are times when witnessing our self through the eyes of others can be a powerful tool in helping us clarify the truth of who we are. His words inspired me in giving myself permission to remember my own declaration of power and self-respect. The

Lesson 8 - Banzai

five-year version of me never doubted his capabilities, nor did he ever question them. They were part of who he was, and he knew it. Perhaps his changing course in order to satisfy the version of himself that others envisioned shifted the grounded confidence in himself. Constantly dwelling in another's opinion of yourself can only yield another's opinion of you, which hardly ever turns out to be steady footing for the longer journey ahead.

Perhaps the biggest lesson I learned was being grateful for what I had. I was on Broadway in the Lion King, the biggest and baddest to ever land on the Great White Way. I also recognized that I had not always invested in the character as a unique individual. Instead, I relied on what I had done and achieved, all the way screaming for someone to validate my efforts and wanting more when I already had enough. And I was enough, with or without Banzai.

    I am more than what I have done and accomplished.

    I am more than what others have said about me, whether favorable or not.

    I am more than a job or a degree.

    I am more than my family, my race, my culture, my religion, my gender, the color of my skin, creed, and any choice I have ever made.

    I am more of who I am, even at this present time.

    I give myself permission to go on a journey to discover the truest essence of myself and become more of what I thought I could ever be.

"What you are looking for is not in the visible or what you can see. It's what's in the invisible that you are after."

- Michael Beckwith
spiritual advisor

On my way back to the east coast, Michael Beckwith made plain to me what I was seeking to manifest in my life. His words helped me create a clean slate and allow what I had already experienced serve as a jumping off point to leap further into my desires and dreams.

Lesson 9

The Listener's Guide

Life is full of jump-starts. When it seems as if we have run out of gas, something or someone comes along to propel us to try again and keep going—even when it takes guts to face it.

Ever since I can remember, I have been inspired by a certain theme of encouragement to keep doing what I thought I couldn't complete. Even within the vast imagination of my youth, at times I experienced a temporary disconnect from a task I desired to finish. It could've been the lack of proper tools, or a search for the right person to collaborate with that seemed to thwart my endeavors. This usually lasted for a short period time. Sooner or later, I'd leap back into a whim of creativity to foster a new idea that would carry me to the end of that to the beginning of another.

In 2005, I was asked to do a performance at Riker's Island Correctional Facility. Riker's is considered one of the toughest correctional facilities in the United States, currently housing young men and women above the age of eighteen. Nestled between two New York boroughs, Queens and the Bronx, the facility is located on an island in the East River. There is a long bridge that leads there.

Upon arrival you must go through an obstacle course of secure entries. At each stop, we were greeted by officers with queries, "Where are you going? ... Whose permission do you have to be on these grounds?"

Finally, once inside, and after all my belongings were scanned, I had to pass through a security device before being allowed to enter the facility halls. This was my first time performing at a prison and I was amazed and its size. I proceeded to the gym, which was transformed into an auditorium with seating for seventy of their male detainees. Unlike theatre venues with dressing rooms and holding stations, I had to use the men's bathroom to change into my costume. Once dressed, I sat on the floor in the hall and watched the attendees file in the make-shift performance arena.

After being given the cue, I walked onto the "stage" and began my presentation. For the first few minutes most of the audience seemed to be interested in the story. However, about fifteen minutes in, a restless mood settled over the crowd. In one corner of the room there was a gentleman talking to his neighbors. I attempted to continue performing in the same vein that I started, full of vigor and passion.

Performing a one-man show is no small feat. This genre of theatre is not comparable to performing with a full cast. What distinguishes this kind of performance is that one-man or one-woman is the show. It is you and only you on that stage creating the tone, personalities, traits, and seamless transitions between characters and scenes—and everything else that goes into a stage production. The energy needed to pull the weight of such a performance is immeasurable. This is enough to caution even the most riveting actor.

Midway through the show, one noisy group had caused the distraction of another. I was trying to keep forging ahead with the performance, despite the growing banter between two different groups. The chaos was starting to feel overwhelming. I decided to do something I'd never done before in my acting career. I said, "Excuse me, gentlemen. I'm sorry, but I cannot continue with people distracting the performance. Concentration is a big part of keeping the integrity of this important piece of literature alive. I will not compete against you discussing things that have nothing to do with what's happening on the stage. Right now, everybody's attention should be on the presentation. Thank you for your time. I must stop for now."

I was deeply disappointed to say the least. I was at one of the most pivotal points of the script. The details of what were about to happen in the presentation would cause an impulse of someone to be inspired by the story. As many times as I had performed the show, I would always be moved by the words and fortitude of the piece. I knew if I felt it, the audience would as well. Nevertheless, as a performer I had promised myself never to be at the mercy of a disrespectful crowd. It is the key indicator that my services are neither warranted nor valued.

    Just as I was about to pull the last prop from the stage, I noticed a hand waving a couple of rows from the stage. Not knowing what to expect, I asked the gentleman if he had something to say. In an unfeigned tone he responded, "I was listening." I took a long pause. Struck to the core of my being, it took me a few minutes to process, and then feel how his words had pricked my deep disappointment and subtle failure. The tone in which they were spoken gave me courage to keep the light inside my heart glowing. Words so poignant that they would alter a non-negotiating rule I'd held since setting out as a performance artist. I responded by hastily resetting the props and reassembling my costume. I felt like that kid again, who for a moment had disrobed of his superman cape, suddenly lifted by a simple measure of words. A feeling of renewal coursed through my body, and the generators restarted with full force.

    My ability to hear the message under this audible cue was a key element in finding the source of playful desire that allowed me to endure. The familiar signs and wonders that I welcomed as a five-year-old were showing me the way, once again. This wellspring helped me keep it moving, and it is what keeps me going today, despite feeling stuck sometimes. My job is to continue expecting these breezes of brilliance to move through and show up at the doorstep of my mind. When they arrive, I oblige. They simply say to me, "Tag, you're it." And I'm off to the races once again. The jump-start that his words gave me that day was not only vital to my performance at the prison, but it would continue to fuel my unfolding career. When what you love to do and create seems to hit a wall, in a moment of seeming forfeit there is something that calls you to come forth and continue once again. This is the match that lights the fire of our deepest desires, causing the flame of life to burn a little longer. There is always more than one way to look at what may be staring you in the face.

"It's not what you get;
it's what you take care of."

- Clarence N. Holt

These words were spoken by my father as a way of inspiring me to be thankful for what I had, as well as a reminder to be responsible.

Lesson 10

You Can Run but You Can't Hide

As soon as I finished settling the rent with my new roommate, I placed my belongings in my room and bolstered outside to my new city. I made my way to the street corner, and in what felt like the most empowering moment of my life, I raised my arms to the sky in thanksgiving, realizing what I had envisioned only a couple of years prior. Standing at the edge of 87th Street and Columbus Avenue, in exaltation, I raised a toast to myself for making such a brave move, and to not having to deal with my father again. "I am far enough away from him that his words can never haunt or hurt me again," I claimed. I would find out that my words could not be farther from the truth.

After being in New York a month, I was cast in the national tour of Jesus Christ Superstar. After a two-week run of the Northeast, we headed to the Midwest and then the Mountain West region. We were riding on a sleeper bus, blazing through Wyoming in the middle of the night after a performance, on our way to the west coast. I was exhausted and went immediately to my bunk to sleep after the show. After a couple of hours of rest, I decided to go to the front of the bus and sit. Our bus driver was always eager to talk, so I engaged him. We began the conversation by talking about home and the places where we were raised.

"Do you know much about your ancestry," he asked.

"Well, my mother is a quarter Cherokee. She has shared with me quite a bit about our ancestors. I don't know that much about my father's side of the family, though," I replied. "Well, my wife does a lot of research on all kinds of people and where they're from." He went on to tell me that she'd made some interesting findings based on facial features. I'd always been interested in the ancestry of my father, since Dad and I had many similar facial characteristics. As a child, people's response to seeing me with my father would always be an immediate comment on how much I looked like him.

"Boy, you look like your daddy spit you out!"

As I grew older their words became grating. The suggestion that I looked like him at all became insulting to my ears.

He continued explaining how and why he had made the observation. As I listened, I made a slight turn with my head to look out of the window. A strange object blew parallel to the bus and after a few seconds, I finally figured out that it was a tumbleweed. I'd never seen one in person before. Suddenly, as I was watching the tumbleweed roll by, a vision of my father's face slipped into my focus. Startled, I quickly looked back inside the bus and returned to my conversation with the bus driver. But I still wanted

Lesson 10 - You Can Run but You Can't Hide

to make sense of what I'd seen.

Slowly, I turned again toward the window and saw out of my periphery the same apparition making its way into full focus. I met my father's face. All my past began to surface.

What are you doing here? What have I done to you that would cause you to haunt me like this? Leave me alone! I thought I left you back in Nashville where you belong, I wondered silently.

There was no response from the human-like face staring back at me. I took one last, hard stare into the soft eyes of the apparition before returning to my bunk to rest.

Still on our way to the west coast, we stopped at a diner to get some needed food. As the driver settled into a parking space, the rest of the cast on the bus began rustling from a long sleep. I, on the other hand, was still restless from my encounter. I'd tried to sleep, but all I could do was toss and turn, trying to figure out the meaning of what I had experienced. Every direction I turned I saw that face looking back at me. It never spoke a word, yet its focused gaze was more than unnerving. At every corner, in every place, the image or the essence of my father would show up in the strangest of places and happenings.

My mind had been fixed on several interesting experiences that had occurred while I was out on the road. These events followed me all the way back to New York. All of them centered around a painful relationship with my father. I sat on the edge of my bed in my apartment in Harlem; my mind bombarded by the impulses to call him. I knew the reason I was being summonsed. "Forgive him," the voice compelled. "I can't do that!" "He will win if I give in." The urge to pick up the phone would not yield its grip. But it wasn't my mind being counseled to call as it was my heart that was being pulled to reconcile. I picked up the phone and dialed my parents' telephone number. Hearing my father's voice on the other end of the line caused me to panic. His monotone style held so much power. All the memories came streaming back to my mind in a flash. It seemed all the courage taken for me to make the call faded into a seeming vacuum of nervousness. I began with verbalizing the list in my mind of all the ways in which he had offended me. "Do you remember when you said this to me? Do you remember when you did that to me? Why wouldn't you come to see me play this? When did you ever care about me doing that?" I let him have it. In the middle of my rant, I heard the strong voice cut through my relentless rave. "Tell him. Tell him the reason why you're calling." I tried not to listen, but I yielded. "I forgive you, Daddy." There was a pause on the phone. In my mind, I thought the least he could do was respond. He said nothing. This infuriated me. Impassioned, I began running down the other list, recounting old wounds and bruises. In the stream of my frustration, the voice spoke once again. "Tell him what you've always thought about him." "Go ahead; say it," the voice admonished. Determined, I trembled through a force of tears. "Daddy, I love you. I always have and I always will." Without my father saying a word, the call ended. I cried myself to sleep. In the middle of the night, I woke up to a voice. "Congratulations!" "Congratulations for what," I responded. "You did it." Rehashing the phone call, I said, "I didn't do anything. Nothing was changed. He hardly said a word, and the conversation ended with me sadder and more frustrated." "Yes! Everything was accomplished. The forgiveness was not for your father. The forgiveness was for you."

    I tried not to be forgiving. I tried to throw reconciliation away. I tried justifying my stance in resenting him. However, the energy and compassion that was prevalent in my five-year old self had surfaced to speak loudly the truth of my knowing. I couldn't forsake the willingness to seek harmony with my father. Younger 'Charles' never sought justice through bitterness. He allowed things to roll down his back without getting stuck in the mud of resentment. Calling to forgive my father was a first step, and one of the most important decisions of my life.

    It wasn't until later in my childhood that I learned how to accumulate debts and hold others responsible for my pain. Though I scorned my dad for things I thought he left unfulfilled in our relationship, the years of conscious forgiveness and reconciliation broke the spell of a lasting bitterness toward him. I released him from the walls in which I held him imprisoned. When I threw away the key to my disdain toward him, I freed myself as well.

Lesson 11

Don't Get Stuck in The Mud

When we receive the call to go back and revisit a relationship that may have seemed out of sorts for a while, the invitation to stretch further into the true essence of your being is at hand. It is daunting and quite uncomfortable, yet it is necessary for growth. And it's not just about one individual—it never is. The fuller meaning of the experience is revealed when the fruits of reunion are manifested. The power of such an encounter becomes a force of nature, giving all involved the push to become more of who and what they are.

In 2007, my father was diagnosed with end stage renal disease. At the age of eighty, he started a rigorous dialysis regimen. My mother, who was also aging and slowing down, was very capable in helping my father manage his schedule, while also making sure that he received the proper nutrition. Three days a week would weaken the healthiest of candidates. I still marvel at how strong my dad was for enduring the strain on his body. After witnessing my father's physical strength and resilience, despite his diagnosis,

In 2010, I decided to drive from Los Angeles to Nashville for work. With engagements in cities like Nashville, Memphis, Atlanta, Chattanooga, and Arkansas and North Carolina, I filled my calendar with a couple of months of work while supporting my family with domestic chores.

Spending several weeks with my parents offered my father and me a pathway to bond—something we had never learned to do in the past. A tumultuous relationship while growing up thwarted any attempt at becoming close with my dad. Part of the triumph I felt in moving to New York City was due to the fact that there was more physical distance between the two of us. I had been gone from my parents' nest since I was eighteen. Months after graduating high school I was off to college. After leaving the South for New York, my visits became less frequent. Once I made the move to the West Coast, I struggled to make it back home. I tried going every Thanksgiving, but sometimes I was not able to do so.

The reunion of 2010 was special to me. I needed to be under my parents' tutelage – in their classroom yet again. I needed to feel the weight of their wisdom. I had changed, and my parents had as well. There wisdom had continued to grow, and I was ready to step into their classroom. Instead of feeling as if I was there to make up for lost time, I felt like I had dropped back into place, perhaps as if I hadn't missed a beat at all. Learning from these familiar sages was exactly what I needed. Some things never change, and that's okay. Perhaps my learning from

Lesson 11 - Don't Get Stuck in The Mud

the way my mother and father were currently demonstrating their entry into older age was enough knowledge for me to process in accessing my own understanding of self. Things had slowed down drastically for both of them. But I believe that's where most of my learning stemmed from, observing how they seamlessly navigated the shift. The way in which we live our lives eventually slows down. It doesn't mean that we do not progress and become better. It could possibly indicate that we slow our minds down long enough to see, hear, feel, taste, and touch the goodness that is all around us in a greater and profound way.

Much had changed, yet many things remained the same. At times during the day, I would go outside to the front yard and walk around the areas of my childhood playground. There were countless games of baseball played in that space. I would pretend to be every member on either team, both offense and defense. My imaginary friends were not only my teammates, but also the spectators in the crowd cheering me on. I touched the tree that was the base for our neighborhood hide and go seek games. I ran the imaginary bases. Back when I was five years old the distance between each base felt like a mile wide. But now it seemed so much smaller as I was able to cover from first base to home in a matter of steps.

As I headed back inside, I noticed the plaque of an American Eagle next to one of the house shutters. My father was a true patriot. After serving in World War II, he'd become a staunch supporter of America, the country where he was born and the country he loved. These memories were now part of my journey back to the place I was born and raised.

The Invitation

A couple of years later, once again I had the opportunity to make the sojourn back to Nashville. My father seemed to be well within the rhythm of his schedule to the dialysis clinic every week. Up at 4 a.m. to catch the transit bus, back at 11 a.m. to sit in his room and recover. I too had learned how to keep the machine of travel and performance oiled. Out early Saturday morning, back every Sunday night. We were each trying to manage our own life.

My father described his schedule as tedious. I would see him put his head in the palms of his hands. He would steady and look at me and then shake his head. "I don't know how I wound up in this predicament," he'd say. I believe it baffled him how a man who had seemingly skated through life without a health challenge could suddenly find his life held at the mercy of a blood cleansing machine. I'd never seen my father take anything other than an aspirin for a lingering toothache. Now he was taking twelve different pills in one sitting. I noticed my dad had begun physically slowing down even more. His personality was also softening. The van that transported my dad to and

Lesson 11 - Don't Get Stuck in The Mud

from the dialysis center would arrive at 4 o'clock in the morning. Like clockwork, he'd return home at 11. To share the responsibility, I would allow my mother to rest while I assisted daddy. This morning when he arrived back home, he seemed a little spryer than when he'd left. "They pull me so hard," he'd often say, referring to the force of the machine as it purified his blood. He handed me his blanket and proceeded through the kitchen, down the hall, and to his room. As I slowly followed behind him, I noticed some of the thoughts running through my mind. It was hard to believe that a man who'd been the picture of health and self-sufficient his entire life was now frail and dependent upon everyone around him. Always a man of fine stature and a stance of pride, my father was now bent over at a much shorter height, almost equal to mine. I could hardly believe it. He continued shuffling along, and then suddenly came to a halt. I moved closer to ask if he needed to grab something from the kitchen before going to his room. Before I could say anything, he made a swift turn towards me and said, "There's my baby, daddy love's you." I was in complete shock. I was speechless; I hadn't a clue how to respond. My mind began to race. There was part of me that was in utter disbelief that my father had waited all these years to say what I thought he should have said years ago. "Where were those words when I was growing up. I practically begged you for affirmation and validation my entire life. And now you wait to tell me that you love me?", was my first thought. The sting of my disappointment carried a familiar bitterness. Though I had called and verbally forgiven my father in 1997, I was still holding many of my feelings toward him on my sleeve. Like an old stick in the mud, I was distraught and unwilling. For some reason I refused my father's emotional progress, desperately wanting to hear him tell me that he loved me but banishing the thought that those words could ever come out of his mouth. As a child I held my father in high esteem and wanted to be just like him. I watched everything he did. I wanted to be just like him when I grew up. I didn't know a great deal about who he was at five years old. But I was aware of how much I loved and honored him when I was that age. Part of the confusion was that I grew up believing that I never received back from my father what I so desperately wanted: love. In what seemed a split second, I saw through the eyes of my father a soul full of readiness. The question was whether I was prepared to meet him where he was. Then I remembered the other conversation that was happening in my mind. This was the voice that was in alignment with what I had always thought and felt about my dad. It was the truth. It was directly connected to my father's willingness and readiness to embrace the relationship that had been on hold for years.

  We both stood in the middle of the kitchen. His frail body still bent over his walker, and the biggest grin on his face. I, holding my breath and then bravely releasing it,

Lesson 11 - Don't Get Stuck in The Mud

looked him in his eyes and said, "I love you too, Daddy." It was one of the most difficult, yet Soul searching moments of my life. There were decades of wanting to tell him just what he meant to me as a little boy held within those words. And though the dreams of us becoming fast friends faded over the years, I could not doubt the eternal love I'd always felt for him was now in full bloom. Both of us standing there with the biggest smiles on our face. And the generations before us basked in a healing that could only come through a heart full of love.

    Within a couple of weeks, my dad and I seemed to find time to catch up on lots of things. He would dominate our conversations, talking about his childhood and growing up in the South. He loved talking about his experiences at war. I would listen, my mind traveling a mile a minute trying to recreate the scene from the enthralling story he was telling. Many times, I could see him in the frames of the movies and stories playing in my head. My father was a good storyteller, but it was his body posture and mannerisms that were most telling.

    The stories I was able to capture came through inflections in his voice, the slight twitching of his lip, and the quiver in his strong Southern lilt. He would often take a breath and stop in the middle of his tales. What he was sharing seemed to be catching up with his emotions. His eyes would swell with tears. I would take conscious breaths, making sure I was supporting him by being present, even in his emotional realizations. This was a remarkable time for both of us. I had never witnessed my father shed a tear, except at his mother's funeral. And then, he quickly caught his breath and wiped the tears from his face.

Something powerful was in motion, and it was just happening without a force or push. It had been taking course over a period of time. Perhaps this great reunion was giving both of us cause to visit that part of our relationship that was ready to not only heal, but to give us individual freedom in continuing to become the best of who and what we are.

End stage renal disease is what the doctor called it. I could not fathom how an eighty-year-old man could face a diagnosis of kidney failure head on and begin such a grueling course to stay alive. I am not sure that he could either, but he did. One Tuesday morning, my father met me at the table for breakfast. He peeled back the shell of a boiled egg, and gingerly prepared to take a bite and then paused. "I like talking to you," he said in a heavy whisper. "Why do you like talking to me, Daddy?" I asked. "Because you listen to me."

My father loved talking about his time spent in WWII, so I took the opportunity to prod. "Daddy, when you were in the war did you have friends who were killed while in battle?" He responded, "Yes, I did." "Did you feel any emotion? Did you cry? Did you want to cry? Did you feel any sadness? Did you feel anything?" I queried. His answer to all my questions was, "No. I didn't know how to feel. Crying was out of the question." I wanted to know more so I asked, "After you were out of the war for some years, did you ever cry at a close friend's passing?" He said, "No. It was a fight in itself trying to muster up a tear, even then." "Why do think that was the case, Daddy?" And with conviction he responded, "Cause I was numb to all of that stuff." That "stuff" referred to all of what he felt, and the landscape of his emotional being. He continued, "There was nothing and nobody in my entire life that had ever taught me how to be with emotions. You just didn't deal with them. Back then people thought all of that carrying on made you weak and scary. Back then you couldn't be scary 'cause you had to survive. I didn't think about my feelings. After a while, whatever emotions I had—if I had any at all—seemed to go away," he said.

This statement was groundbreaking in my understanding dad's knowledge of his emotional state. However, the operative word "seem" is what I came to know as the biggest falsehood about emotions and feelings in general. We all have them. We were all born with emotions; however, like my father, we don't all seemingly have an opportunity to constructively commune with them. He spent most of his life never having a relationship with his own emotions. Like generations, my father was not allowed the permission to have his emotions to co-exist with the rest of his affairs. This lack of understanding of the range of our emotions affects everything, especially relationships.

Thanksgiving was approaching and my mother called me to go to my father's room to see what the commotion was all about. "Hurry up and go in there and see what's wrong with your daddy. Something is troubling him," she said. As I entered his room, I noticed that he had a Kleenex box in his right hand, and the entire stack of tissues in his left hand. He was sitting on the edge of the bed, rocking back and forth. His eyes were red from crying. Tears streamed down his face. "What's wrong, Daddy?" I asked. He looked up at me. "I had a dream about my momma this morning," he said. Fighting through the tears, he stated, "I want to go see my momma. I'm ready to see my momma." He began to cry and rock even harder. I did not how to handle it. I took a deep breath and heard within, "Stand right there with him. Support your father. Be with him like he has stood with you." Stand, I did. After about ten minutes of furious emotional release, my dad began to calm. He said, "You can go on with your day. I'm alright now." I stayed a few more minutes for his assurance. As I got ready to leave, he said in a most endearing and gentle way, "Thank ya, son."

The Initiation

Thanksgiving came and went. Shortly afterwards, I

Lesson 11 - Don't Get Stuck in The Mud

made my trek back to Los Angeles to celebrate Christmas and bring in the New Year. I was particularly grateful for the experiences I had with my dad during the time spent in Nashville. With the month of January ending, the rest of the year looked as if it was setting into a normal flow. During the final day of the month, my sister called me early to inform me that dad had to be taken to the emergency room due to a serious bout with back pain. There was an urgency in my sister's voice that I cautioned to. Without taking too much time, I purchased a one-way ticket to Nashville and headed out the following day. During the entire flight, I could hardly think about anything except the relationship my father and I had crafted over the years. Most of it had been tough and emotionally painful. However, the last couple of visits home had been some of the most fulfilling and happy of times in my life—just because I had a chance to spend time with my daddy.

The lengthy journey had caused my arrival to spill into the evening hours. The only meal that I'd had was a smoothie before boarding, and I was starving as I stepped off the plane. I arrived at my parents' house and immediately jumped into my mother's car and headed to get some food. My plan was to settle in for the night and head out the hospital in the morning. However, a soon as I made a right turn out of the driveway, an inner voice instructed me to go see dad right away. All the way to the hospital, I thought about the images, which had been haunting me.

Lessons From My Five-Year-Old Self

My mind was inundated by messages from the past. Although they seemed to disappear in a flash, I knew they held within them valuable information. The scenes spanned the emotional spectrum. The common denominator was that most of them contained painful episodes that had been too tough for me to digest in my earlier years. But now I noticed that, even in this full, vivid state of remembrance, the sting of yesterday's pain had far less effect on me. Things of the past seem to fade into the burgeoning relationship between my dad and me.

During the next couple of days, I watched the nurses attempt to make him feel as comfortable as possible. I could see that he was in a great deal of pain, although he was not fully coherent. The only time he made a sound, which sounded like a painful grunt, was when a nurse repositioned him in bed. His breathing changed drastically. The lapses between breaths became longer. Although he didn't exhibit any abnormal change in skin coloration, as many patients with his condition do, things had been made clear. Dad's body was shutting down. My sister would comb his hair and make sure he was presentable for visitors that came by. My brother, who stayed in denial of my father's condition until the last few days, eventually came in to give him an encouraging rub on his hand and forehead.

One evening before others had arrived, I went to sit with dad. I wanted to begin the process of saying goodbye.

Lesson 11 - Don't Get Stuck in The Mud

Though my father had rallied many times, giving us hope that there remained the miracle of him pulling through, we all knew that he would soon surrender and leave us. I believed that although he was seemingly incoherent there was a part of him that could still communicate.

Gazing at my father in his bed summoned the fond memories of tracking his every move as a child. Now, watching the man who I so desperately wanted to be like take his final breaths was surreal. I had once again become that little boy who, though staring at a frail body void of vitality and strength, knew that he was in the presence of a giant. I was occupying the space with a legend—a brilliant man, full of integrity and wisdom, who had done his best and completed his course on the planet.

The poignant memories of my father rushed to mind. His smile and all the possibility I held for us in becoming fast friends. I couldn't help but think of the toil and pain of trying to get to know one another. But I reveled in knowing that in those final few years we caught up as best we could. I came to understand that it was the five-year-old who would always hold a light in the shadows of what seemed to be wrong. I was once again that eager child that held the light—this time for my father and for myself. Both of us were entering a world of the unknown—an adventure that we were both preparing to take.

"I love you, Daddy. It's okay to leave," I told him gently. "I want you to know that I will hold all the lessons you taught me deep in my heart forever. It's our covenant to one another. I'm so proud to be your son. Everything is all right, Daddy. We are going to be okay, and we sure are gonna miss you. But I know that you're all set for your next journey. And you are ready to see your momma."

    I knew, we all knew, that dad was making his transition. Yet I was stunned ... for what reason I still don't know how to articulate. The eminence of death eludes being managed. Its sting of reality is what we cannot regulate or calculate. That moment was overwhelming. No more waiting for that phone call. The anxiety and sadness were fading into the infallible beauty and truth of life—my dad's life eternal. The following day my father passed, releasing his mortal coil and any need to hold on to this world. He returned to his eternal self. I entered a new initiation of life by existing on the earth place with my father's physical absence for the first time.

    That one moment in time, which seemed to linger in my mind as well as my body, is what I will remember most. On one hand, I was sad to the point of tears. I hated to see him go. On the other hand, I felt relieved because he wouldn't have to battle his failing physical condition any longer. No more the need to measure vitals, or accumulate data, or record statistics. Dad had been released. "You did it, Daddy. You passed all your tests with flying colors." He was completely free again.

Lesson 12

Surrender to the Truth of Your Heart

During my life I had never been reluctant to move about the land. From Nashville to New York City in 1996, and eight years later another move, this time to Los Angeles. Since 2005, I had been on a mission, travelling across the country singing and speaking at churches and schools. Boosted by a letter of recommendation from the founder of Agape International Spiritual Center, Michael Bernard Beckwith, I was on the phone every day trying to convince musicians and directors to allow me to be a part of their Sunday service event calendar.

My first gig was in Santa Barbara, California. At that time, I was driving to every event location. I didn't have the money to buy airfare, and my weekends were spent coursing the freeways of California and neighboring states. A couple times each year I would be treated to a flight to perform in Oakland. I traveled as far north as Sacramento and as far south as San Diego, hitting all places in between. Soon I began making the four and eleven-hours road trip to Las Vegas and Salt Lake City. My cousin Darron was always a joy to be around, and I would spend a few days with him while he was completing his doctorate degree at University of Utah. Then I stretched east to Phoenix, and then to the Pacific Northwest. Portland was always one of my favorite places to visit. Seattle, though a much larger city, had beautiful traits of its own; however, Portland's charm always kept me coming back. Many trips to that area were designed during the academic school year. Fall can be particularly beautiful in that part of the country. I would book an event during the week at an area college or university, and on the weekend my schedule was filled with church performances. With a vast list of contact numbers, I had learned a vital element of crafting and booking my own work and schedule

It wasn't too long before I'd booked enough events to nearly fill an entire year of weekends. And with a steady stream of income, I could finally afford to purchase airfare. This expanded my travel as well as my vision. I was able to cover larger areas and go further distances. In addition to moving to venues beyond the West Coast, other directors and music ministers began requesting that I share my talents with their congregants on Sundays. I obliged. Mile Hi Church, in Denver, was one of the late additions on my schedule, but it quickly became one of my favorite places to visit. The band was stellar, Dr. Roger was always on point with his message, and the community was genuine.

    After "winning" the West, I dipped into Texas and nearly stayed. It wasn't that I was a big fan of the state,

Lesson 12 - Surrender to the Truth of Your Heart

however, the number of venues that welcomed me could fill at least a month of dates on my calendar. Between Dallas, Houston, and Austin, I could set up shop for at least two months, performing at different churches and schools during the week. Very seldom did my events line up for me to spend time in one place for an extended period, but I still made my rounds in the Lone Star State quite often.

Although I had vowed to plant and stay in Los Angeles, the impulse to move hit me like a wave. Part of me could not see myself leaving the matchless weather and rays of the western sun. Yet something was weighing heavy on me. I couldn't quite reckon with it. That was until it started to become emotionally and mentally painful. It wasn't a physical burden; however, the need to continue to grind and push my way through was excruciating at times. I would get messages from my higher mind stating that there was work to do elsewhere, that L.A. had been vital and necessary, yet a temporary stop on my journey. I sifted through memories. I took careful survey of all twelve months. I thought about what had transpired, and I allowed myself to brave the flash of the most memorable occasions—the good, as well as the challenging experiences. A weighty sum of pondering memories, of making my rounds through the city's landscapes would make for interesting conversations as I began to usher in a new beginning and mark the ending of another.

New Year's Eve I was sitting on the corner of my

bed, listening to the fireworks outside. The entire city was celebrating. As in previous years, I had shut everything off, including my cell phone, and lit a candle to begin my ritual of taking introspect. My first thought was to pray aloud, but I chose to keep silent and allow my focus to slip into slow breathing that I often found in moments of mindfulness and meditation.

I gave significant thought to all that came up, and then I started releasing those things from the past, many of which I was more than happy to say goodbye to. I needed time to unravel the cord. A cord that winded through a rainbow of emotional shades and colors. A cord with knots and twists. A cord that snaked down unknown roads into valleys and peaks, and moments of bumps and pure bliss. A cord that continues to unfold as my life.

"We are pushed by pain until we are pulled by vision." Michael Beckwith poured these words over the congregation like honey over oats. Although I'd heard him say the quote numerous times during his Sunday morning talks, I didn't take to the message initially. Although generous with my desire for others to understand it, I didn't realize the depth and wisdom of my spiritual teacher's broadcast with regards to my own life.

    It had not dawned on me how drastic my life would change in the few months after hearing Beckwith's citation. In the summer of 2015, I had more than a notion that my life was on a course to another major shift. I thought it

Lesson 12 - Surrender to the Truth of Your Heart

was a passing fancy when I first felt the urge of this message, but a relentless pop-up of visible signs, along with constant broadcasts coming through morning meditation, were enough to convince me. The impression left on my Soul from these encounters let me know that I was being ushered into a tempest of change.

In hindsight, I see all of this was the making of a perfect storm. My seemingly comfortable world was falling under siege of a swiftly approaching tsunami. A steady boardwalk of work at correctional facilities, schools, and churches along the highways of cities and countryside was being splintered into pieces, like my thoughts. Lucid dreams, that I could not explain, haunted me. The harder I pushed to make things happened, the harder life pushed back with stalled attempts and midstream malfunctions. "Why aren't things working out like they usually do," I shrieked. I grew restless and irritable, becoming more despondent by the day. This was all in addition to a severe creative drought.

I couldn't see the full view of what was taking place, though. I had resolved to the convenience of how my life had out pictured for a decade—keynote speaker, avid traveler, singer, producer, author, and workshop facilitator. Nothing seemed wrong with this illustration. But I was out of sorts, and to some extent out of steam, yet being swooned by an undisputed desire to be a trailblazer on the forefront of emotional literacy, self-worth, and healing through forgiveness.

    I had been sitting on a volume of material collected through years of talks, visits, and discussions with groups around the country on the experience and navigation of emotional pain and hardship. This initiative was birthed through an account with an intensive study of my collection, and subsequent behavioral patterns—all stemming from an emotionally painful journey with my father. I was also longing to go back to New York City and resume my career as an actor. It had been over a decade since I'd left the stage, and I was ready to go back to the Big Apple for another rendezvous with performance on the Broadway stage. With an inner force pulling me in the direction of this important work with emotional literacy, coupled with a constant craving to sing and dance again, I was confused. How can I have two seemingly different yearnings pull at me at the same time?

    This was enough proof that I was preparing to experience an inevitable reposition in my life, and that I was easing out of my fixation to my complacency. But I obviously underestimated the weight of my past in my own mind. Messages flashing through my thoughts, and images that repeatedly stretched my eyes of appearances won my attention, and my vote to stay right where I was: Look at what you've already created. You're on a roll! Stay right where you are. Yet, there was another witness. It saw beyond what my surface eye had observed and previously recorded. It saw what was possible; a world that had not yet manifested but edging to be birthed through me. This inner guide and watchful eye held vigil, while my Soul tracked the light to my truth. This gave me space to glimpse how my life was unfolding. However, this glorious peak into my greater yet-to-be did not calm the raging tides inside; it seemed to tempt them even more.

    The situation was becoming increasingly unsettling. My resistance to what I knew in my heart became the culprit of my growing anguish. I tried justifying my defiance by packing on dates and events to my calendar—staying busy and staying put. I kept reasoning that I could not function properly without my daily dose of the sun's vitamin C and Runyon Canyon's hiking trails, two of the most treasured aspects of living in Los Angeles.

    At last resort, I used my church as an excuse. There will never be another place like Agape Spiritual Center. I used all kinds of different ways in trying to validate my point of staying under the western sun. But even reasoning with the value of my beloved spiritual community could not convince me to continue to run from the vivid broadcast of my innermost being. Still not willing to heed the trust of my inner knowing, I deepened into fear and depression.

    I needed a lesson on remembering how to lift myself out of what felt like a swamp of distress. There were consecutive days in bed with my entire body covered with sheets and pillows. The brightness of the sun that I'd come to depend upon was starting to make me dizzy. I literally felt like I was losing my mind. In desperation for support and guidance, I called upon my chief advisor, Michael Bernard Beckwith. "I can't seem to find my balance in all that is going on in my head," I said in a tone of upset. "I have two different dreams that I can't seem to manage. I want to do another Broadway show, while at the same time wanting to share my curriculum on emotional literacy and learning with the world." I went on and on explaining, blowing like a windbag.

In the middle of my rant, he interrupted. "They are not two different things; they are the same. There is no difference between the two except for what you call them," he revealed." I stared at him waiting for a more detailed explanation to what he'd just said. And he returned the stare without saying one word. Ok, I guess he's done, I thought. But I was still puzzled. "How can they be the same thing?"

"Don't worry about the detail, that is not your responsibility," he answered. "Follow the Truth of your heart. It's calling you, and you get to follow. It leads to your next assignment. Just surrender to It. Let go of all your expectations and how you think it should look." I took a deep breath. He continued, "At this point you really don't have a choice, Charles. You know your divine mandate is going to have the final word. Surrender to your truth, young man. Allow it to lead you." I took another deep breath. "Go back and get it," he said with a quickened tone. "Go back and get what," I asked? "You already know the answer to these questions, Charles," he ended. What is it that I should let lead me? I thought I had already gone back to get it. What is he talking about?

"We love you and are always praying for you."

- Mrs. Martha Patton
church Mother and neighbor

One first Sunday morning church service, during the ritual of The Right Hand of Fellowship, Mrs. Martha's words penetrated my young mind and connected to my heart. I knew she meant what she said, and I never forgot it.

Lesson 13

Provision Comes with the Vision

There is no doubt that one thing leads to another. Whether it stems from a thought or by an action, we are always in preparation for something to shift. It doesn't matter if we are conscious, or asleep, change is happening. And change is good.

It didn't matter what I had created in my mind to do. I knew that if I could see it happening, the provision and all that was needed for it to come to fruition was already in place. The size of the vision is not a problem. Sure, it may take some things longer to manifest and become reality. However, the fact that you can visualize a dream coming true is enough to germinate the provision that allows the process to take place.

This experience was tied to a trip to Nashville, when the last house my parents lived in was being sold. Although the house was vacant, I felt a strong ancestral pull to be there. This house stood on a parcel of land that my father grew up on. Even more important was the fact that this same piece of land was connected to the lot where my beloved grandmother's house once stood—the place that had helped mold my development from the beginnings of my childhood. The place where I imagined things that became realities. The place where big dreams were born. Yes, indeed, I needed to be there to walk the grounds, to witness, to reminisce, and to experience powerful feelings that had launched my creative imagination. A few days would give me enough time to complete this sacred tour, I thought. And just like that I had an insight. I sprouted an idea of sharing my curriculum on emotional learning with Nashville public schools. I had no immediate desire of implementing the program. I was on a mission to get back to resume my career as a Broadway actor, and I didn't want anything to stand in its way. However, I thought having the conversation could set the collaboration in motion for a future return.

In late Autumn of 2016, I called to set an appointment with the Nashville-Davidson County Board of Education. They directed me to the top executive officer of student support services. Unbeknownst to me, the person I would be meeting with turned out to be a gentleman with whom I attended high school and played varsity football. Both excited to see one another, we talked for a while about our lives and careers before discussing my reason for coming. Shortly after I began detailing my curriculum, he made a phone call. While I was still explaining the program, he interrupted me. "You have a meeting next Wednesday with a school principal who has an interest in implementing your project."

Everything was laid out to me by the principal in

Lesson 13 - Provision Comes with the Vision

our initial meeting. He dotted the I's and crossed the T's, covering all the expectations. I agreed, knowing that my program would fit the school's desires well. He then explained that because my program had not accrued enough quantitative measures by the board's standards, they would not be able to pay me until the completion of my third month. This was a bit disappointed, but I was still on board, viewing the initial three-month period as a 90-day trial to show that the curriculum would be a benefit to students as a pilot program. The principal vowed that in the meantime a budget would be created to continue the program and pay me for my services, if we all agreed.

Afterwards, he took me on a tour of the school. "I've done pretty extensive research of your work, and I think your program is a perfect fit for what we're trying to achieve," he stated. Still in somewhat of a daze, I kept asking myself if I was considering postponing my second act on Broadway in order to do this. It all happened so quickly. One week I'm talking with a student support executive; a week later the principal of an elementary school and I are discussing which days I will be working in the classroom.

After our visit, the principal and I agreed that we should have one final meeting before the Thanksgiving and Christmas holidays. It was during this talk that I confirmed my decision to work with the kids on emotional literacy and learning beginning the next semester. I was excited and scared at the same time. I never intended to stay in my hometown for more than a couple of weeks, let alone an entire semester. My goal, after leaving Los Angeles, was to stop in Nashville to take break from the road long enough to gather myself for the remainder of my drive to New York City. But I knew that I was being called to stay from a force much greater than my dream of being back on the Great White Way. I took a deep breath, knowing my dream of returning to New York was not being delayed, and that my return would not be spoiled.

Now that I'd made the decision to stay, I needed a place to live. With my parents' home being sold, the prospect of a temporary living situation did not exist. But I chose not to focus too much on where I would be living. My efforts were in creating a safe space where my program could best benefit the minds and lives of youth, helping them create a healthy emotional existence. My focus was on the benefits of the program. I knew the opportunity to teach students vital skills and virtues that would influence their lives and those around them was a rare and remarkable opportunity. I knew this was mine to do, and it made me feel good. I lived in that vibration with no worries whatsoever.

One morning I was reading through my Facebook messages and ran across the name of a childhood friend who I'd not had communication in years. This was a great surprise, as she was one of my best friends in elementary school. We exchanged telephone numbers, and after a brief

Lesson 13 - Provision Comes with the Vision

conversation, we decided to meet for coffee the following morning. During our reminiscing, she questioned about what project I was working on, and what had led me back to Nashville. As I updated her, she asked, "Are you living here again?"

"Yes, looks like I will be moving here to implement my program," I responded. I continued to tell her about the special prospect that I had been given. She too was elated. "Where are you going to stay?" she asked. "I don't know, but it will all work out somehow," I responded. I felt confident that I was on my true path and that Nashville was where I was supposed to be, and I confidently shared that with her. Donna took a quick drink of her coffee, and without hesitation said, "You're staying with us." "I'm staying with who?" She said, "Our daughter graduated college a couple of years ago and we have an empty bedroom that has your name written all over it, Charles." I was stunned. "Are you sure, Donna?" "I'm absolutely sure, my friend," she quickened.

A few days later I arrived at their front door, John, Donna's husband, and her son, who was about to enter his last semester of high school, greeted me with open arms. Their dog, Autumn, gave final approval to my reception. "You are now a part of our family, so make yourself at home," Donna said warmly.
Within a week's time, I was all settled in. My bedroom was on the second floor. Although it was above the living room,

where most of the family activity took place, there was a near deafening silence in my room. Sound rarely penetrated when the doors were closed, often making me feel as if I was living in the massive structure alone. The room had an interesting feel to it. It was cozy, yet with a hallowed sense. I often felt that I was inside a covering, a cocoon perhaps.

One of the most powerful realizations happened during the first week. While in meditation, I became overwhelmed with gratitude for seemingly no reason. In years prior my feeling of gratitude lauded the expectation of things that were attached to a specific outcome, to those things that existed in the past, or possibilities that were connected to the future. However, my current consciousness didn't carry any of those conditions. I was fully present to the gift of life that was available to me in the present. Everything I desired was wrapped up in the immense, sacred impulse of the moment. It was all that I had; it contained all that had brought me to that point, and all that would unfold—without the slightest focus on the past or the future. This was one of the first times I'd experienced such a profound move of complete trust in myself and in the Universe.

What a revelation! I didn't expect Nashville to be more than a temporary refueling, nor did I think my opportunity to employ my project would be this immediate. But I was confident this type of work was needed, and I knew I was called to do it. I was given a grand opportunity to serve the lives and trajectory of youth—to be a beneficial presence to those that will one day govern our world and society. This gave me a heightened feeling of gratitude – one that hasn't been rivaled since.

"It will be revealed to you,
just keep going, Charles."

- Lissa Sprinkle
dear friend, confidante, and spiritual guide

I would sit for hours talking with with Lissa in her office. She would listen as if what I was saying was the most important thing in the world. She would then share her timeless wisdom and counsel.

Lesson 14

Manifested

In January 2017, I was introduced to a group of third and fourth graders: fourteen rambunctious young men in high-spirited chatter and loud laughter, who were chasing one another around the room. "This is Mr. Holt," the principal yelled, trying to reach above the volume in the room. "He has come to teach us some important things about mindfulness and how we can be our best." As the room slowly calmed down, the principal continued with his introduction.

The principal suggested to me that the group of young men he had selected would feel the greatest impact of the program. "They can be a little rowdy, but their potential for excellence far exceeds any behavioral issue," he said. "I have complete faith in their capabilities." I could tell within the first few minutes of speaking with him that he was invested in the success of each student. I knew that working with these students was exactly what I was supposed to be doing. I tried denying it, but the joy I felt inside gave me full confidence that this assignment fit perfectly in the core of my alignment. I coordinated my plan with the principal's vision and began working to help them win. I went through the curriculum with a fine-toothed comb and vowed to stick to the detailed plan.

We began by sitting in a circle, creating a feel of community rather than a conventional classroom. I was hoping to reinforce the importance of human-to-human communication, connection, and response, amid a high-tech society the young men had become used to. I purposely engaged each student, acknowledging his presence; allowing him the opportunity to acknowledge mine. We proceeded. "Take a deep breath in ... and release. Listen to yourself take a deep breath in ... and release. "Notice how it feels in your body as you take a deep breath in ... and to let the breath go," I instructed. After ten deep inhales, on the last exhale I said, "Hold it, hold it. Now, with a big exhale make a silly sound. GO!"

You can only imagine some of the sounds that the students made. While they laughed at their outbursts, I gazed around the room. Although I had crafted a syllabus, the level of effect and retention would only be beneficial if I allowed the students to teach me how to facilitate. I too was now ready to be student again. Class was now in session.

The first week we spent covering the basics of mindfulness. Focused breathing was the theme of the session; checking in on our feelings was the order of the day. "How are you today?" I asked. A few responded, while the majority sat silent, shrugging their shoulders. This was a helpful clue in what direction to move in. It was obvious that

Lesson 14 - Manifested

a lesson on literacy would be highly valuable. Students' ability to give language to the ways they feel is imperative in beginning the work to recognize and navigate emotions.

By the end of the second week, we had covered two of the program's most important principles: respect and balance. Nearly every young man was willing to share at least one word on how he was feeling. We talked about our feelings and how we determine what respect and balance mean in our everyday lives, and most importantly how they were connected to the way we respond to our emotions. "What if we are not feeling happy, Mr. Holt?" "We are not going to feel happy all the time. That doesn't mean we take our unhappiness out on someone else, nor does it mean that we have to stay unhappy. We should never allow the way we feel to influence our respect for someone else," I responded. "Respect always begins with yourself," I reinforced. Getting young men to understand self-respect is sometimes not learned through lecture. Putting principles and tools into action is a good way to improve retention. One of the fourth graders raised his voice while stating, "Never be mean to someone else just because you might be having a bad day." From that day on I never doubted the potential of a child—or anyone—to increase vocabulary and knowledge. The students were quickly catching on. This delighted me, giving me a feeling of worthiness, knowing that I'd created something that could be added value to the life of another human being. My vision manifested in ways I could hardly explain.

Although the group had initially been reluctant to share, I was encouraged when students started to feel safe enough to comment. As one student chose to brave the waters of conversation and begin to talk, it usually served as an icebreaker, creating a snowball affect into group discussion. As they talked amongst themselves, I became an observer. "I was really scared the other day," one young man said. "I was scared too," chimed another. Soon the entire room agreed on how they felt as a result of a severe outburst from a couple of their peers the week prior. "The craziest things happen in the cafeteria," one third grader acknowledged. They all sounded off in concurrence.

Later that afternoon the principal approached me and said, "My students have come to me telling me how 'Mr. Holt is teaching us mindfulness, and how to listen to our breath, and how to respect others, and how to stand in our power.' I would be overjoyed if you could stay the remainder of the semester. I am confident that we will find the funds to pay you for your remarkable work," he added.

How It's Beaten Out of You

I was happy that my efforts were being acknowledged and felt. But I admit, the past few weeks had been some of the most stressful. Getting the young men to say anything about emotions or some of the ways in which they felt, was like pulling teeth. However, at times I was surprised at their broad ability to demonstrate compassion, thoughtfulness, and intuition. These flashes of innate expression were not always the case, and sometimes few and far between. It took time for their seemingly tough exterior to dissolve. I understood the way in which they felt and their dilemma, how could I not. Much of what I witnessed resembled the markings of my emotional trials at eight and nine years old. Their hard covering was a way of protecting their feelings and learning to resist and dismiss emotions they had been taught run from.

The resistant behavior is one of the foundations of becoming emotionally vacant. As a naturally sensitive young man, fighting back emotional expression was a cultural and gender code I had to endure through my youth. As males, we were and still are taught to be strong and tough, highlights of being seen as masculine. Shedding tears was not part of that agenda. "Crying was for 'sissies'," they said. This conditioning was instituted and reinforced by older males. The act of crying was deemed a sign of being weak, and it was the last thing a boy or his father wanted him to be labelled as. Sure, there were other ways of being branded that held high stakes in the stamping of masculinity. You had to be careful of the colors you wore, who you chose to associate with, what hairstyle you wore, and what sport(s) you played. Sports were king in pinning one's level of masculinity and acceptance. Playing contact sports like football and boxing kept in with qualities and codes of conduct that protected you from suspicious and judgmental eyes. However, there was something about a young man crying that made some older men take notice, and others cringe.

    Boys are taught not to cry at an early age. Boys who cried were labeled as being soft and fragile, like girls. This still applies, and its repercussions are lasting. The impulse to address our emotions has been beaten out of us by this type of relentless circumvention. I witnessed a student's father chastise him over the young man's feeling of failure and subsequent outburst of tears. "Stop all that crying, or I'll give you something to cry about," the father yelled! The young man desperately tried sucking up his disappointment, violently wiping the tears from his face. The father grabbed the young man's hand, whisking him out of the doors of the school to their car. This touched me. I remember those exact works coming from my dad when I was in the third grade. I was eight years old, and our baseball team was up for the little league championship. The score was tied 4-4 in the last inning. The opposing team had runners at third and second base, and all they needed was one good hit to send the runner on third to home plate. We were holding secure with two downs; a quick out would give us another round at bat to hopefully take the lead and win. That was until the batter hit a ground ball to me at shortstop. I was ready to field the ball, when out of no-

Lesson 14 - Manifested

where it took an unexpected bounce, causing me to fumble it. As soon as I picked the ball up, I heard the roar of the crowd. I looked up and saw the other team at home plate jumping up and down in celebration. I put my head down and began to cry. My teammates who were disappointed as well surrounded me to console me. As I made my way to the parking lot after the game, my father was there waiting. "What is wrong with you," he asked? "We lost the championship, and it's my fault," I explained. Shaking from crying so hard, I rolled the window down to let the breeze dry my tears. It was then that my father began yelling at me. "Stop all that crying, boy. That makes no sense, you carrying on like that," he squawked. I couldn't stop crying and I couldn't bear the sight of his face. To lose the game was one thing, but to feel the insult by the person who I thought never seemed to care anything about what I participated in, was an even harsher and crushing blow. I cried despite him yelling at me, to the point of having a headache. But something drastic took place in my young mind of reasoning as a result of that encounter. My father was the most influential and authoritative figure in my life and his words rang loud and thunderous like a drum, luring me away from a vital and innate expression. The stain of his verbal punishment for crying caused me to become resistant to expressing my emotions. From that day on, whether my father was present or not, I paused at the thought of releasing through tears. Swayed in my opinion, I too began to believe that crying was a manner for the weak. After all, if my father insisted that I not cry, then I should make every effort not to.

Once I started the gradual divorce from my emotions and feeling tones in my youth, it wasn't until I had a meltdown in Midtown Manhattan that I began to ask myself questions. I was thirsty years old and feeling the heavy weight of my feelings. This was important, as it gave me the ability of learning to manage and navigate the hardship of emotional trauma. However, it took years to muster the courage to glance at my feelings again. Like a movie of my life playing in my head, I did not want to engage those frames. A burst of tears amidst the frustration and fear seemed to give me a needed sense of clarity and helping direct me back to the path of my emotional grounding.

Crying is an emotion, and a vital one at that. The emotional body is part of the whole human experience, and not having the ability to find the language or expression in learning how to describe or demonstrate how you feel it is like not having it at all. There was a lot for me to sift through. The question I gave my attention was why I felt and behaved certain ways in the first place. All things have a beginning, a place of initiation. Whether it is learned behavior from a parent or from an event that travels with you everywhere you go. When a student is asked "why?" they feel the way they do, the burden of emotional illiteracy bears hard on the ability to respond at all. This creates frustration, therefore leading back to the detour lane. Avoidance of the topic altogether yields nothing except a deeper well of misunderstanding, and what I call the emotional by-pass syndrome – something I struggled with for many years.

In The Room Where It Happened

I asked the school principal if I could spend time in the cafeteria during my students' lunchtime. The principal agreed. I knew this would be a great idea. More time with them made me less of a visitor, and more of a member of the school community. Plus, lunch time is where what is left unsaid and suppressed is vocalized, manifested, and revealed: all in the cafeteria. It's the room where much of what happens outside the schoolhouse is shown in full scope.

As a consultant, I wasn't allowed to directly ask students about their domestic situations. I steered clear from any questions targeting the behavior within their family and its affairs. But, as I observed things play out in the cafeteria, my interest of understanding their life at home was illuminated through their behavior. Observing these actions could give me insight in understanding different types of emotional trauma and the effects on a child's behavior, their ability to learn, and possible trajectory. The cafeteria was the room where all this took place.

The ears of listening cut through the chatter and noise to reveal what may be demonstrations of behavior that lead to long lasting habits, and the initiation of patterns that could lead to future distress. When I began working with students, I found that some lacked even a remote opinion about their feelings and emotions. A shrug of the shoulders was a standard response. Others would respond "good." That answer I found to be part of a growing condition of desensitization, and lack of self-esteem. Some would not respond at all, as if something inside of them had completely shut down and frozen up. Very seldom did I witness this, but when I did, I found it to be quite puzzling and daunting. One day I sat across from a second grader. She began eating her lunch, seemingly pleased with her food and what she had chosen from the lunch buffet. I turned my back to her and took a scan around the room, making sure that the other students were finding their way to their designated tables and seats. Suddenly, I hear screams and wailing from someone behind me. I turned around to find the young lady, who I had witnessed just minutes before, in full distress. "What happened? What's wrong, I asked?" She bellowed even louder, trembling in her seat. I tried consoling her for the next few minutes, but she continued in her suffering. As I tried to figure out what could have possibly taken place, I noticed that her eyes were in full focus, though not at me. I looked over my shoulder to see if there was a person or figure in her view.

Lesson 14 - Manifested

Nothing and nobody were there, however, she continued her hypnotic stare. I finally realized that her gaze was not fixed on anything in the room. Seemingly frozen in time, her bellowing stopped, and she finally blinked her eyes. "Can you tell me what happened?" "My best friend left me to go sit next to somebody else at the end of the table, she whimpered." "She's not supposed to be sitting with her, she continued." She rambles on, "She left me. She left me because she doesn't like me anymore." I interrupted her before she could add more volumes to the story. "Just because your friend left to visit another friend doesn't mean that she is not your friend anymore, and it doesn't mean that she's not coming back." "Yes it does, she snapped!! She began to bawl once again. Startled, I waited until the young lady calmed before speeding to the principal's office, explaining to him what had occurred.

Fight and flight played out quite often in the cafeteria. Students would resist the rules of conduct by the lunchroom attendant and buck up against authority through verbal and physical demonstration or by dismissing themselves and hiding in the halls. However, the complete physical immobilization and suspension of any type of reaction, I had not witnessed since I attended elementary school. I realized the young lady's attention had been stolen by the intoxication of a trauma related incident that had not been initiated in the school cafeteria. The chilling encounter with a seven-year-old was a prime example of how an event begins to mentally and emotionally distress the mind into containing memories of traumatic events that trap you in a state of emotional reactivity. Trauma of any type has no bounds concerning gender. When left untreated and void of discussion, the conditioned programming that it leaves on our emotional landscape can be debilitating. When triggered, its residual fallout can toxify an environment. After the incident occurred with the second grader, I asked the principal if we could begin including girls into the program. He agreed.

Lesson 15

Imagination is My Superpower

As I opened the door, a burst of energy nearly blew me over. I'd heard the raucous banter all the way down the hall but had no idea that it was spilling out from my classroom. "What is going on in here?" I mumbled. As I quickly scanned the room, I noticed the class was engaged in a myriad of activities. In one corner was a trio of young ladies playing the Rock-Paper-Scissors game. A few others had settled in the middle of the room, to practice their skills with multiplication cards. My eyes were astonished. My ears, however, were drawn by the excitement and the high pitch of four, excited young men in a far corner. This seemed to be a very constructive use of time, without the guidance of an instructor. Before I could set my attention to another corner of the room, a fourth grader reached out and grabbed the sleeve of my shirt.

"Mr. Holt, you've got to see what we are doing over here." Still trying to adjust to the sensory overload, I hurried over to see what all the commotion was about. "Watch this, Mr. Holt." The young men had drawn, cut out, and glued together pointed hats. They put an elastic string through holes they carved out to secure the hat to their head. Each put their cap on and began pretending to be a rocket ship. What genius! I watched in amazement. From where had they come up with this idea? How could they have created a missile from a piece of colored paper? As I had begun to marvel about how these young minds had come up with such a concept, I felt another tug at my arm. "Put it on, Mr. Holt. Let's see you become a rocket ship!" Without hesitation, I obliged.

I strapped the nose of the missile to my head, and signaled with an enthusiastic, "Okay, I'm ready for take-off!" I jumped up once. I jumped up a second time, and the third time they all jumped with me—pretending that we were all lifting off into outer space together. As I looked around, I noticed that we were each in our own creative world, being held in the same orbit of this creative genius.

This hat was more than a colored square sheet. When it was put on as a head piece, this piece of paper was activated into a superpower – one that could launch you into the cosmos. Through imagination, this became our reality. After the students let for their next class, I sat in the empty, quiet classroom. Memories of my childhood began to flood my mind. I could remember when my level of fresh inventions soared like the sky—when the whim to jump right into a moment of fantastical imagination and bliss was far from being silly, but rather a force that made living in the moment the greatest thing ever. Where did all of it go? When did I begin to sacrifice the impulse to create something out of nothing in a moment's time to deem-

Lesson 15 - Imagination is My Superpower

ing the very act as childish and absurd? In deep thought, I realized it had been around the same time I settled for copying things from others. I'd spent years dismissing my own brand of make-believe brilliance by settling for beliefs handed down to me. Had I forfeited my own genius? I never doubted that I had the gift of imagination; I always knew I did. I still recall having a spectrum of inventiveness as vast as the universe. My world of discovery was impulse for creating something out of nothing. However, the courage to access it, or the willingness to allow it to be a spontaneous course stalled at times and weakened over the course of years, so I thought.

    I worried if my creative mojo had left me altogether. I wondered if I still had a hint of this wondrous ability—the one that had so magnificently been demonstrated through these fourth graders—an ability to bring something from an imaginary world into a reality. Though the demonstration of the rocket ship was more metaphysical for me, the conclusion on which I'd arrived was that I always had the capability of being my own launch pad, igniting myself into a world of imaginary genius. My move to New York to be on Broadway, and then becoming an author and inspirational speaker were prime examples of this creative charm that I'd easily forgotten. The one from which this exercise had originated was yet another of many examples. From a piece of paper, I could transform myself into a rocket ship and fly through outer space!

To answer my own question, "Where did my imagination go?" I knew I had to return to when I first believed. When I was five there was nothing that I could not achieve. I put it to task every chance I got because I made possible the opportunities to do so. When it seemed as if I was in a place of being stuck, I allowed my imagination to create a way in which I could release what felt like was holding me down. I found it easy to glance beyond the eyes of appearance and see what I could become, even when I could not fully articulate or comprehend it or the way it made me feel. Something magical happened for me at that young age: I appreciated and up leveled the ways in which I saw life. I was thanking for what I had, although I desired more. I appreciated the source from which I had received. Gratitude was the bridge that carried me to the next blessings. With what felt like a cosmic jolt, my entire body was filled with the ecstasy of possibility. Anything was imaginable, likely, and achievable. Imagination became my superpower.

Things Being Made Clear

The important things I wanted to experience were made manifest in my life. From academics to sports, from listening to the radio with my daddy, to asking my grandmother to fix me a peanut butter and jelly sandwich for lunch. I'm not saying that I had everything easy. Believe

Lesson 15 - Imagination is My Superpower

me, I made great efforts in fulfilling the responsibilities I was given, and I completed them with excellence. That was the manner in which my parents raised me. They held me in check, and they also understood that I needed space to grow and unfold in my own way.

I am grateful that my parents exposed me to all types of characters and types of people. Television personalities like Flip Wilson, band directors like Lawrence Welk, and an assortment of blues musicians. My community, Lake Providence, also had local celebrities who could stand with the best of them. Our little town's self-proclaimed griots would present story and song out of nowhere. Each talent brought with it the gift that made what I saw a vibrant bouquet of the fullness of life. Everything I witnessed became a new palette of possibility from which I could paint my life. And all of what I created and experienced would in some way be a vehicle of inspiration for others.

This new assignment was no different. I realized that I was there to give back to these young men things I had learned through the years that had served me—manners, respect, self-worth, perseverance, mindfulness, forgiveness, courage, creativity, and confidence. It wasn't that these young men did not already possess these qualities; however, I could see they were not being nurtured in a way that would allow them to continue to dream their rocket ship dreams. Most of them did not have the support of two parents at home. They were not surrounded by elders and sages who created a ground for them to learn self-respect through the respecting of others. Instead, many of them made speedy paths to their homes in order to escape an invitation to gang activity or a stray bullet. These young men were not championed with words to encourage them, even when they failed. I was showered with: "That's alright, get up and try it again. You'll make it, just keep trying." They instead heard words condemning their efforts before even starting. Their attempts to become a better version of themselves always took a back seat to a reminder of a time in which they'd failed. Most of the young men in my class had mothers who made them feel inadequate. They bullied them with words, making them feel they would grow to be like or worse than their absent father, a failure. How did I learn this from my students without ever asking? In the cafeteria. The cafeteria is the place where the honesty of a child's emotional state of mind is revealed. But this kind of talk and behavior wasn't anything new. I had grown up hearing rants of this kind from the parents of some of my close friends. I'd even heard it from the lips of my own who, in trying to make me comply to their rules, yelled out words they wished they could retract. These, often public, displays and tirades of casting down of the child continue to offer the most destructive effects on self-esteem and self-worth. These types of words clip the wings of impulse to dream. Their influence on the psyche usually manifests into behavior and action that continues

Lesson 15 - Imagination is My Superpower

to reinforce the pain initiated from the beginning, causing a battery of charges against self-discovery and healthy relationships.

My vision was becoming clearer. I knew from personal account that a lack of emotional literacy could cause unimaginable disadvantages. I'd tasted the spoiled fruits of poor, unhealthy relationships too many times. I wanted to create a space where the children could explore and understand their own emotional grounding, while learning how to manage and navigate its hardship. But it wasn't all about a curriculum or mastering a way of teaching it. My assignment was about inspiring a way of life in which these young men could become aware of the opportunity in giving themselves permission to live a successful and happy life. Being able to give language to feeling tones and the understanding of emotions was a vital component of this tutorial. I could not grant this for them, but I could help them visualize a way to experience a desired life that, with a fundamental grasp of their emotional landscape could thrust them back into the capable consciousness and stream of their genius imagination, despite a hiccup or prolonged detour to their path.

I came to share with these third and fourth graders the virtues from a lifetime of my own lessons and detours, hoping to inspire them to their best. They had come with a wellspring of wisdom to offer me too. I made myself open in listening to and witnessing messages being conveyed under the tongue and beyond the eyes of appearances. Ultimately, I wanted that we all would feel like we could win.

Lesson 16

You Got This!

What does a child want as he begins to find footing in the new landscape called the world? Who could a child call on to speak the words of support as she begins to learn and embrace the landscapes of life? Where can a child turn when a brand, new beginning can be confusing and without civil instruction? Who can be the familiar face and confiding energy that, even when we fail, calls us back to posture by standing in the gap for us in the meantime? Who can champion the vastness of our imagination through our desires and hopes, though, sometimes farfetched and without reason?

Everybody deserves to hear the voice that rings loud, even when it seems like things are hopeless and that our dreams are gone. That's what my brother was for me. Oddly enough, in his absence I can see more clearly the lush panorama of blessings he bestowed upon my life. I believe our relationship was consecrated long before either of us landed on the earth plane. It was by divine ordination that our paths would cross and intertwine as such. He was in my life to show me and reveal an unconditional love. I was there for him as a student, someone that would listen to him, to respect him—somebody who would take his words as genuine, and as worthy. He shows me still that I am well kept, in the best of hands no matter where I am on my human path; that my life continues to unfold in a magnificent way. My brother showed me that I was a treasure in his world. I hope I somehow showed him that he was a treasure in mine too.

As I write this manuscript, I see my brother's face. I hear him cheering me on as I learned how to ride a bike for the first time. I hear his instruction amid screaming fans during a Friday night football game. I watch him as he goes to talk with the coach on my behalf. I feel his heavy arm around my neck during my time of disappointment, comforting me. I see his joy as I become better. I pierce his eyes as he admonishes my behavior. I feel his strength as he hugs me. I see his eyes shut as his body lies still in the front of the church's sanctuary.

    My brother was my parents' first born. He lived with them during their elderly years. My brother was close to both my parents. My mother and brother were also best of friends. They talked at least three or four times a day, even while he was out on appointments. Approaching ninety years of age, she would often say that her day was only complete after my brother had made it safely back home after work. There was nothing he would not do to please her.

    In the fall of 2018, my brother's health began to rapidly decline. Stubborn, like my father, he thought he could

Lesson 16 - You Got This!

manage his health without the aid of necessary measures or being under a doctor's care. My brother's eating habits were not in alignment with the doctor's dietary restrictions. In fact, he seemed to eat every type and style of food the doctor admonished him to refrain from. Within a matter of weeks my brother's poor health standing turned from bad to worse, and he once again wound up having to go to the emergency room. This time, he was fighting for his life.

Unlike previous trips to the hospital, he had no alternative but to stay to be under close monitor. For nearly two weeks of daily checkups on his condition, I became exhausted from feeling helpless during his rapid decline. My sister spent time traveling between her home in Atlanta to the hospital in Nashville. My mother was living in Atlanta, close in distance to my sister, under the care of a senior facility, but made sure that somebody from the family was at my brother's side. Along with my brother's health, there was growing concern regarding our mother who was nearing her 90th birthday. Since they were so closely bonded, his health had a direct effect on her emotional and mental well-being.

After unsuccessful tries to stabilize his condition by his team doctors, my brother slipped into a coma. My brother had too many physical issues working against him. Despite his will live, his vital organs began shutting down. He fought to stay alive, but the inevitable was at hand. When my brother transitioned, I thought it to be more of a blessing than anything else. I hated to see him go, but I did not want him to suffer any longer.

After receiving a call from my sister confirming his death, she thought it would be best to wait until she returned to Atlanta to tell our mother the news in person. I agreed. I prayed all day and night for peace to surround my mom, knowing she would be in a well of sadness. At her age, the slightest bit would put a strain on her entire body. I did not want her to falter.

Prior to my brother's passing, I was scheduled to fly to Los Angles for a couple performances. It happened that my brother passed the night before my scheduled flight to the West Coast. I debated not going before finally deciding to keep my word with the event coordinator. I knew that my brother would have insisted on me carrying on with my commitments and doing what I love to do. I stayed two days, which was long enough to fulfill one of the two events.

I felt a growing need to be with family, especially Mom. I ended up taking a red-eye flight to Atlanta. It took about four hours before we landed. Though exhausted from the emotional distress and a physically demanding schedule, my only intention was to make it to Atlanta safely in order to surround my mother with every ounce of love and comfort I had. The next few days were spent preparing the funeral services. Before making it back to Atlanta, my sister and my brother's son had begun the process of completing the details of the funeral by handling some of my brother's personal affairs.

Because we had chosen to have the memorial on a weekday, we decided that mid-day would be better than evening. As we arrived at the church, I noticed the faces of people I had not seen since I was a child. A remnant smile, a distinctive laugh, a unique stroll, or a particular body posture revealed enough for me to make the connection, even from many years of distance and not being in contact. This gave me, and my family so much joy. There were enough hugs and heart-warming laughter in that place to light every city street in Nashville. Close relatives, friends, and the immediate family made the journey to Nashville to say good-bye. The weather was severe in some places along the way. Flash flood warnings had been in effect days before of our arrival. The forecast for the day of the service was more moderate, yet rain was predicted again. In our hearts, however, there was a ray of sunshine for our brother. The vibration of love was everywhere. I felt like I was five years old again.

My brother, Clarence, nearly fourteen years older than me, had friends come from all over to pay their final respects. "Your brother was a good man, and one of Nashville's best at getting your drains and pipes unclogged." Holt's Drainage was a familiar name and business all over the city. One of my brother's oldest patrons commented, "He was one of the best in the business," someone said.

"Yep, Clarence was my go-to guy whenever I had a problem," chimed another. Named after our father, my brother was a man of his word and an incredibly talented and hard worker. He never stopped at good enough. "At the end of the day, your responsibility is to make sure the customer is completely satisfied," he'd preach. "Otherwise, you don't have a craft, and you won't have no business either."
On February 15, 2019, my brother passed away. On February 22 we would lay him to rest. It all seemed like a dream. At one point during the family visitation, prior to the funeral, I consciously removed myself from the line of visitors and all the happenings around me. I sat back and silently witnessed with the eye of the observer. I stared at the body in the casket and realized that what I was looking at was merely a shell. The mortal coil, vital, yet temporal, had ceased to function and exist as a living thing. However, my brother was much more than something as finite as a physical body. He was a life force, something that could never die.

My Best Coach

My brother was a master at getting the best effort from me. His coaching skills were key to my success as an athlete. His approach to instruction was firm, but always constructive. When I was five years old, I was enamored with George Foster, the right-handed slugger for the Cin-

Lesson 16 - You Got This!

cinnati Reds. I wanted to be a great ball player just like he was. "Come on," my brother said, "Let's go get you a glove so you can start playing baseball." He took me to Nashville Sporting Goods and bought me the best mitt they had. We then took it home and oiled it down to help the leather loosen a bit. We went outside and he began teaching me how to field and catch the ball. After that, he bought me a bat. I preferred the aluminum bats to the wooden ones because I loved to hear "ping" when you made a solid connection with the ball. We spent countless hours playing catch.

At his discretion, he would take me to the batting cage so I could sharpen my hitting skills. I wasn't the tallest in the bunch, but I could hit a baseball a country mile. After a couple of trips, my brother thought it would be best for me to take batting practice with him as pitcher rather than a machine. His efforts paid off. I became an all-star baseball player. However, after playing the game since the beginning of elementary school, I decided to trade in my baseball cleats.

During my seventh-grade year, I became a track fanatic. My brother, who was not as big a fan of the sport as I was, was still a key motivation. Coach Fred Hill became my fondest coach of any sport, as well as a track mentor. The 100 and 200 meters were my specialty. I also anchored the 4x100 relay. Coach Hill stuck me in the long jump as we approached the city championships. He always believed I had the ability to be a world-class sprinter. My brother sanctioned Coach Hill's thoughts and began putting me through sprinting drills at home. He realized that my greatest weapon in any sport was my speed.

As I entered high school, my life seemed to be centered around sports, and an undeniable passion for football. Noticing this, my mother began intervening. She established a mandate, "If you're going to be involved in school activities and play sports, you have to get just as involved in church." The parents of my friends had endorsed rules as well, like my mother's. They felt that our being in the choir would consume more of our time in something constructive, and less time to let loose the wandering minds of coming-of-age teenagers. With limited options to choose from, my friends and I chose to join the young adult choir, known in the area as the Echoes of Jericho. This was our way of balancing things out, in favor of our parents. Since we all played the same sports, attended the same school, and lived in the same neighborhood, holding each other accountable would be an easy chore.

We had choir practice for a couple of hours every Saturday, even on dates we would not be the featured choir on Sunday morning. This took dedication. But we stuck to our commitment to attending choir rehearsal like we did going to football practice. The Echoes of Jericho had a special blend. With over sixty voices, our melodious sound seemed to cause the heavens to open and shower

Lesson 16 - You Got This!

down blessings everywhere we sang. Me and my friends, although none of us claiming to be vocalists, bolstered the tenor section. The closest I had come to training was when I stayed with my grandmother. But it wasn't as much about the music as it was the feeling it gave us singing side by side and knowing that we were all on one accord.

By my junior year in high school, I'd become one of the most recognized running backs in the city of Nashville. College football programs began showing interest in my talent and invited me to their campus for weekend recruiting trips. When you go on an official visit, it's always during a weekend when the school hosting you is playing a home game. You would arrive on a Saturday morning before kick-off. Time before the game started, you'd spend meeting the coaching staff and the other recruits. Some of the highlights of my visits were touring the athletic facilities, experiencing the game, and getting to meet and hang out with the players afterwards. It was during this time that each recruit would be introduced to the player responsible for hosting him during the weekend. I always had the best hosts, all of them stars on the team. If you were lucky, and the campus was not too large, you could get a tour of the campus to see the academic buildings. If I was interested in attending a particular school, I made plans with the coach to return for a visit during the week while the student body was present to witness the real thing. This made me feel like I was living the life of a collegiate student-athlete.

Recruiting trips were the best. My brother was especially proud that I was receiving attention from some highly touted college programs. His little "project" had blossomed into one of the best. Standing at 5 feet 7 inches tall and weighing 155 pounds soaking wet, I was far from the tallest or the biggest in the bunch. But what I possessed separated the good from the great. Speed was the name of my game. All what track and field had given me in terms of competing against the fastest kids around, prepared me for dashes up and down the football field under the Friday night lights. Before every game, my friends and I would go to the top of the bleachers and scan the field. This was part of our pre-game warm up. The manicured grass and its slightly brownish tint from the relentless Southern heat were like a picture-perfect painting that I could lend my stokes to in a matter of seconds. The smell of football season was intoxicating, amplifying my excitement up to full blast. All it took was a good block and a slight crease for me to slip through the defense. Once I found daylight, I used the gift I had been given to find the goal line. TOUCHDOWN!

Everything I did was for the sake of getting better as a football player. My diet, my attitude, and especially my grades were top priority. My brother never missed a game. Whether it was rushing for more yards, making a great block, and leading my team to victory, each week was a call to get better. Although I knew he was taking notes on my performance, it was a huge boost to my confidence to see him sitting in the stands. We would spend Saturdays watching college football together. For me, it was a classroom. "You see how he gave him that leg and then took it away?" "That's what made Gayle Sayers one of the best to ever play the game!" He'd carry on about the little things that separated the good players from the great ones. "You have that ability too," he noted. "You have what it takes to be just as great as he was." I hung on to every word out of his mouth, believing that what he was saying was the gospel truth. My brother was a student of football, and I became one as well under his mentorship. I believe my brother understood the importance of football. He knew that the sport gave me a feeling of power, something I needed going forward. He was right. Football made me feel invincible in the sense that it gave me courage to tackle any obstacle, believing I would win.

What I Remember Most

Flashbacks of sports and football caused me to rewind the tape even further, taking me back to my childhood and the beginning. I remembered my brother teaching me how to blow my first bubble memories of him giving detailed instructions on how to ground a baseball and how to throw a tight spiraled football ran like an old black and white film coming into full focus. "See how I have my fingers lined up with the stitching on the ball?" "Yes," I eagerly replied. My fondest memory, however, was him teaching me how to ride a bicycle. I don't know why this reminiscence stayed so firmly intact. Determined that it was time for me to take the training wheels off, my brother insisted that I learn to ride free from his assistance before the sun went down. "You got it," he asked? "Yes, I got it," I yelled in response." "Ok, I'm going to let go. You got this!" Going no more than three miles an hour, to me it seemed like we were on the Daytona 500 Speedway. I was terrified, but ready. Then without notice, he let go. As soon as I realized that he'd released the bike, I started peddling for my life. I kept paddling, and I never looked back. As I approached a slight downward slope in the street, my heart began to race harder, and my eyes stretched to the size of golf balls. Oh no! Now that I got this thing going, how do I stop it? I panicked while trying to find the breaks. In a feeling of terror, my fumbling foot finally found traction. I remembered to not brake too fast or hard, slowly easing the bike's pace. After coming to a complete stop, I turned the bike around and rode back up the hill. My brother was right where he was when we started with the biggest smile on his face. Part of that grin was from him laughing at my fright. He chuckled, "Looks like you did good for your first time by yourself." As we returned to our house, he put his hand on my head and said, "I'm proud of you. You did it."

    My brother's affirming touch made me a feel like I

Lesson 16 - You Got This!

had been knighted. I felt like I was on top of the world. He always saw me as a superstar, and he was there to remind me when I slipped from my courageous standing. His confidence in me was a blueprint in my finding the same for myself later in life. He always saw me as the greatness in which I could become - holding the gap until I could gain my own focus. The poignancy of his validation will always be with me, giving me a voice and a presence to speak from my own self-validation and self-worth.

At the blink of an eye, I became aware that I was still in the sanctuary. I took a deep breath, reassimilating back into the room. People and friends were still passing by one last time to say so long. With tears in my eyes and a heart full of gratitude, I prepared to do the same. I thought, besides the memories, what legacy will my brother leave? My brother wasn't a movie star, nor did he have celebrity status. He did not possess a lot of houses, or land, or a hefty bank account. What my brother carried was a life full of character and dignity. I am sure he had gathered a heap of it through pain. Yes, trials, tribulations, failures, and triumphs. Nevertheless, his life was a light to a fulfilling journey that, sprinkled a bounty of benefits on him and those he encountered.

Three traits immediately came to mind: selfless, unconditional, and supportive. Though he was not a deeply religious person, my brother would give you the last shirt off his back. I witnessed him emptying out all the money in his pocket to give to someone whom he did not know but wanted to help. I had many discussions with my brother over the years; some were personal and very close to my heart, yet I felt I could confide in him. I cannot remember a time when our thoughts collided that he did not end the conversation with, "Well, I don't necessarily agree with what you are doing, but you know I'm always gonna love you." I believed every word. I never questioned my brother's love for me. It was genuine and unwavering.

It is every child's dream to grow up with someone who cares so deeply about his or her possibilities in the world - someone to emulate and strive to be like. Every child deserves to have somebody help them stay grounded when situations seem uncontrollable, and the ground unstable. That is what my brother was to me. Every time I get the opportunity to be selfless, unconditional, and supportive, I shall become these attributes, in his honor. He may not be here in form, but he is still teaching me to do and be my best.

Lesson 17

The Force of Internal Rage

Though a very personal account, I believe we all can share stories of how the current state of affairs have caused a kind of craze, sending us thirsting after the same waterhole—the living water of life itself. Feeling exhausted from every attempt to find refuge, we seem to stumble in search of an oasis. Mirage after mirage we become dry, brittle, and dehydrated from the grind and the mental weight of worry, doubt, frustration, and fear. The drought seems to be endless. However, in winding down stream, we run upon a promising sanctuary. This reminds us that the residence of our meltdown is the same place that houses the reservoir where we can quench our thirst and live in the flow of life and be free again.

    I'd experienced this lesson many times before. Learning to deal with a heaping amount of fear and uncertainty started during my early years when I tried to see beyond the frightful darkness of a particular situation in order to see the light at the end of the tunnel. I believe I carried the aspirations to freedom for years, and I would take this concept and hold to it with all my might.

    During the first week of April 2020, I encountered a force of rage that I'd never experienced before. as it consumed the contours of my mind and eventually spilled me into an emotional dungeon. This visit, what I will call hell, spun me into a sixty-minute blight in which I began doubting my very existence. The inspired path I'd been carving for many years began to fold, and I felt the pressure of what I desperately tried to sustain collapse. I landed in a hard, daunting bunker from which I could not run from nor find words to describe. I could only feel it.

  I had finished a run of performances with the Memphis Symphony Orchestra and was looking forward to a couple of days of rest before flying back to Atlanta. On my way home from the airport, one of my friends in Memphis texted me letting me know that I had gotten out of the city just in time before the lockdown. What kind of lockdown is he talking about?

My phone was full of messages referring to what my friend had texted earlier. The President of the United States had issued a State of Emergency due to a deadly, novel coronavirus that was swiftly making landfall and wreaking havoc and tragedy in other parts of the world. I took notice of what was happening because of the possibility of it making its way to the United States, but I did not want to give in to the surfacing wave of hysteria this pandemic had started.

  With a full schedule of events in the coming weeks and months, I kept moving forward with my ear to the ground as the wave of concern continued to grow. I tried processing what exactly was going on and how I was going

Lesson 17 - The Force of Internal Rage

to respond. "What kind of virus could be as devastating as they say this one is?" Soon after the initial information was released, the virus was reported to have already landed on American soil. A surge of destruction in China, Iran, and parts of Europe was cause for concern before its inevitable turn to the United States. Baffled, I recounted my recent return from the two countries, during a string of performances four short months prior. Things seemed normal as could be. Both were now being ravaged by a mysterious flu that nobody could speak clarity to. Italy and Spain eventually issued nationwide lockdowns as did other places. Washington State was the first place in the United States to report a string of cases, along with deaths of those who had been infected. This sent thunderous shock waves through the country. Fear spread with increased talk of the virus making its rounds to the rest of the country. I think for some, particularly the U.S. Government, the stark, trumpeting broadcast had arrived too late.

In a matter of days, the virus took an enormous bite out of The Big Apple, the country's most populous city. The number of cases and deaths mounted with reckless abandon. People everywhere felt like time was running out. Literally. That the end of the world was upon us. Highly regarded officials' tongues seemed to be tied in trying to explain what this virus was and from whence it came. Many Christians proclaimed this event to be the one that would announce the sound of Gabriel's trumpet, calling forth the Bible predicted "end times" and the ensuing rapture.

I tried to make sense of what was happening. The only event of this magnitude I could reference was 9/11. Everyone who was living in New York City in September 2001 remembers it like it was yesterday—the fallout of a tragedy that would forever change the world. Living on 111th Street and Frederick Douglas Boulevard, on a large screen television from my living room, I watched the Twin Towers fall to the ground. Numb and emotionally short-circuited, I couldn't take the overload. I left my apartment and walked a path all the way down to West 58th Street and 6th Ave., known as Avenue of the Americas. It was there that I saw a cloud of smoke resembling pictures I'd seen of the devastating plume of an atomic bomb in history books. It was the most traumatic event that I'd ever experienced.

The world came to a screeching halt for a few days. For those of us in the theatre community, we were notified performances would be cancelled until further notice. We were assured that after the investigation and proper protocols were put in place to resolve what had happened, we would return to our weekly performances. We missed three shows in total before resuming our eight-show schedule of Lion King. Though many theatre houses held at half full, after the show's short hiatus, patrons soon returned in expected numbers. After a month, Broadway and the ma-

Lesson 17 - The Force of Internal Rage

jority of New York City, returned to full flow again. The world was forever different, however. It took a while for the world to adjust, and for New Yorkers to regain their confidence; but it slowly returned.

For this very reason, I thought the COVID-19 pandemic of 2020 would play out the same way. A few days to reckon with a "super bug" until a course of action would cause us to resume as normal. But after two weeks the pandemonium increased to an unimaginable hysteria. City officials were instructing citizens to shelter in place. "Stay at home at all costs if you can. This virus is deadly."

A novel coronavirus meant that there was no vaccine and no knowledge of just how it spread and to what lethal degree was its contagion. Soon after, there was a curfew put in place to assure that people were not interacting with one another. This worry about people being in close proximity was what global health organizations like the CDC feared most.

Amidst the curfew and anxiety that had gridlocked the world, I was beginning to spiral out of my emotional and mental grounding. The last thing I wanted was being cooped up in an apartment alone for most of the day. I had to get outside and at least take a trip to the grocery store and to the park. Every day I would find a few hours to get some fresh air and a walk wherever I could find trees. Their presence offered a vibration that felt like the only semblance of sanity I could find at the time.

One day, during all the chaos, it rained for twenty-four hours straight, with periods of thunderous downpours. I was stuck inside the entire time, from sun-up to sundown. I went to one of the windows and pressed my face against the pane. The news that Broadway had been closed indefinitely rang through a post I read online. Everything around the globe was shut down. The world as we knew it had come to a halt. All news seemed to be worst-case scenario. A feeling of desperation ensued, and I felt myself slipping into a deep well of uncertainty and depression.
Infections were spreading at catastrophic rates. People were dying in record numbers around the world. New York City was quickly becoming the global epicenter of this unprecedented catastrophe. Each day the statistics continued rising. The frontline workers, nurse practitioners, and those holding "essential" occupations were scrambling to push against a growing wall of death and destruction, one that they were fighting to save themselves from as well. New York City inhabitants, along with the rest of the world, were terrified. Questions filled homes and hospitals. Answers seemed most elusive, and the gage on time soon disappeared for many. Days of the week became strangers as if we had all entered a twilight zone.

    What does this all mean? What is trying to get my attention? What am I being called to do? I tried finding empowering questions to ask myself, since feelings of helplessness and hopelessness lingered. I laid awake through

Lesson 17 - The Force of Internal Rage

the night with optimism and gaping eyes to stretch into the promise of a rising sun, only to face another day filled with unbearable fright.
Without any type of cure for the virus, worry, fear, and uncertainty loomed heavy on the minds and hearts of an entire civilization. While sheltered in, it seemed that I could hear something that sounded like an atomic blast. BOOM! My heart would sink every time I'd listen to the media's announcements. Their reports spoke bloom and doom, always with scenarios of the worst possible outcome. In weeks, this loom of uncertainty morphed from a cyclone to a tsunami.

Through all of what was happening, I still clung to hope that amidst all the broadcasts I'd hear a glimmer of favorable news with concern to the theatre. The Show Must Go On! How can the very stage that gives so many people jobs and joy all of sudden shut down? My life is in full expression on a stage. Everything I love to do is on a stage: performing, speaking, singing, teaching and facilitating. It's the one place I can go to share my gifts and talents. It's the platform that has supported me from the moment I, literally stepped onto it. The place that I can let go of all fear, self-criticism, and shame is the stage. The stage has always lifted me up and given me a voice. Now what? During the first week of April, three weeks removed from the initial downward spiral due to the virus, I was in the kitchen washing vegetables in the sink, with a pan of red lentils slowly cooking on the stove. All I could hear in my mind was "Broadway is gone and it's not coming back ... Broadway is gone and it's not coming back..." With every repeat, the volume seemed to increase. This sent me into a mental state of overwhelm. My breathing became heavy with quicker pulses. I felt myself begin emotionally spiraling out of control. I went through an entire landscape of feeling tones, trying to find traction. Though I've never taken medication for anxiety, the downward slide from one emotion to another made me feel like I was under the influence of drugs, trying to find the magic cocktail to ease a wrenching emotional pain.

These feelings were not new, but never had they been as severe and uninterrupted. I was conscious in my ability in naming them. Denial, depression, frustration, irritation. These led to deafening, isolated anger, which brought along self-criticism, self-doubt, and a mountainous heap of scarcity. I call scarcity the "I'm all washed-up drug," and that's exactly how I felt. Like I had nothing, wasn't gonna do nothing, and had never done nothing worth anything. Sinking into a deep sadness, I felt my light dim. This was one of the most dangerous ways I have ever had felt in my life.

As a carrier of light, inspiration, and unparalleled freedom the very essence of who I am was fading under a cloud of fear. I was so sad; I could not cry. I was too numb to muster up any type of tears to force my healing.

Lesson 17 - The Force of Internal Rage

How did you get here? What have you done with your life? Why don't you own your own home? What are you going to do about money? If you'd stayed with IBM you would've been set by now, you wouldn't have these things to worry about. You'd have all the privileges that those benefits would have afforded you. You should have gotten your master's degree. You'd be better off if you were married. I bet you're sorry you became an actor, the most unstable job in the world. And on and on ... The onslaught of self-bashing continued in force. I beat myself up for a lifetime of choices.

After holding court with me, myself and I, I segued into a growling resentment. Then pity and bitterness showed up to the party and I became immersed in full victimhood. Somebody did something to me to cause me to feel and experience life this way. It's all their fault! I started walking through my family to see whom I could blame, and what I could blame them for. Family first, right? My father's face appeared first and then my mother's and sibling's. I thought I had finished peeling off the layers of hurt and failure. I thought I'd conquered the core of disappointment as it concerned my family. But, it wasn't until my own face appeared that I felt an intense scathing; I remember staring at my resemblance as if I were the main culprit.

Part of me was fighting to pull away from that rage. I heard a voice say, "Charles, come back. Surrender to peace, Charles. You can do it." As I was hearing this, an undercurrent of a trauma-induced flood of thought began to swallow me, and my conscious breath left for a moment. I felt like I was trying to find the surface from a deep-sea dive. Finding a small lifeline to peace in that moment, I managed to break the plane. I took a breath. And then a double breath with eyes wide open.

With an emerging soberness, I took a step back from my kitchen sink and immediately picked up my phone to call one of my mentors. I felt embarrassed in confessing I had swung into the depths of rage and danced with its phantoms. I couldn't believe I said the word hate. This vibration was deeply troubling, and I made several more calls before finding my way back to my center.

Still reckoning with the traumatic residue of how these events made me feel, I felt the impulse to look at myself in the mirror. Focused and intent, I heard a voice say, "Wow, Charles, the people who you vilified and accused were not affected by any of your damning fury. You took all of that on by yourself." I had burdened the entire weight of an exhausting rage. The volumes of pain, disappointment, and disdain that I'd created in my mind consumed all reasoning and questioning of my blame's truth. I returned to the mirror in my bathroom several more times, scanning my life. Like peeling back an onion, with each round, I became more than willing to take full responsibility for what had happened and how I had spun out of emotional control. It was in this empowered state that I declared an emotional

Lesson 17 - The Force of Internal Rage

oath, "My life is a good life, and I am responsible for all of it – the way I feel, the choices I make, and how I express my emotions. I don't have to allow anything or anybody to cause me to spiral out of control through a silent rage. I give up blame and any conversation that would point the finger at somebody else." Birthed from this oath came a sense of self-forgiveness. I forgave myself for holding tight to the guilt, the pain, and the shame of not thinking I was enough, while realizing I had done the best I could at that point in my life. I gave myself permission to make missteps as I walk uncharted territory, as I move forward. I was already feeling the strength of this momentum. This process was a genuine endeavor, aiding me in resuscitating all of what I had cast down in that hour's rant. My dreams, my visions, and my expanding life were now being buoyed by a conscious renewal of emotional well-being.

A big reveal from this encounter was confessing to my being a victim. Victimhood was a foreign feeling to me, one in which, as a little boy, I had learned to stay far from, dodging its contagion. I did not make habits of blaming others for the way my life out pictured or for my life experience, instead I took credit for what I created in my experience. I was convinced of what I could change. Those things I regarded as unmovable and uncontrollable, I left alone for my parents to handle

There is a lasting remedy when I find myself in this situation again. I will choose to spiral up to the power within my emotional energy and realize this is the greatest momentum to my happiness. I will remember the gems of wisdom I learned from my parents and grandparents. My ancestor's journey will cause me to smile, knowing that I am the manifested word and deed they did not have the opportunity to voice in the world. I will cause my mind to jog the memories of my giving, my sharing, and the efforts of being a beneficial presence wherever I am.

Lesson 18

In the Name of Jesus

While on the set of a biopic in the city of Atlanta, I sat down and began a conversation with another actor who also happened to be a local minister. I shared with him that I had recently returned from a six-month tour of the Baltic, the Mediterranean, and the British Isles. He asked if I had found a church home and offered his church as a possibility. He explained that his church was of the Baptist faith. I told him that I grew up in a Missionary Baptist church and that during my college years began my path into the apostolic faith, which was a brand of the Pentecostal movement. He assumed that I was still "saved" through the blood of Jesus Christ. "You look like a man of God," he said. "Yes, I am saved every day by the renewing of my mind," I countered. He continued by quoting lyrics to an old hymn that I learned when I was a child, Jesus Paid It All. I went on to share with him the story of my community and how it was founded. "You really didn't answer my question regarding whether or not if you were still saved," he said. "Yes," I quipped, "I told you that I was saved every day by the renewing of my mind." Nodding his head, he looked at me with the most puzzling eyes, searching to see how much truth he could find in my response. I recounted with him my past and an experience that changed the entire meaning of being "saved."

Growing up in the South I had been automatically enrolled in the school of religion. God was above all else and family was a close second, with everything else a distant priority. Since there would not have been a community without the founding church, attending Sunday service was routine. I didn't like going to church so much. My mother allowed me to bypass the 10 a.m. service, but it was a requirement that I attend Sunday school. My parents made sure that I was dressed and ready to go as soon as the doors of the church were open.

Repeat after me children, "In the beginning God created the heavens and the Earth." Our teacher, Ms. Fannie Mae, would always put a special emphasis on the sentence that stated, "And in the beginning was the word of God, and the word was made flesh." She'd conclude with "God is love." Like the rest of the class, I repeated every word she said. But to tell you the truth, the part about the word becoming flesh was Greek to me at my young age. However, there was one thing that I had a pretty good grasp of, and that was "God is love." I knew it to be true because I had seen it work through my parents, my grandmother, and through the elders in the community. More than them ever telling me so, I felt the strong power and vibration of love in their actions.

Being a Christian was everything. Being able to tell

Lesson 18 - In the Name of Jesus

another the name of the church you attended held within it a particular pride and power. On the other hand, if you did not admit to being part of a particular congregation, people would label you a "heathen" and count you out of their favor, and God's as well. Since 1868, my ancestors made countless journeys to the pews of Lake Providence Missionary Baptist Church. Some of the same narrow paths that my parents and grandparents trod were there for me and my friends to walk to the church house. Each Sunday we would wake early and track the soil to praise God, while keeping the family name under the good graces of Jesus, and of course, the sometimes-self-righteous neighbors. We were never pressed to know the Bible from cover to cover but having knowledge of its contents heaped upon you showers of blessings from the neighborhood elders; rightfully so, since the community had been founded by a missionary.

  As learned as I was, some of the stories in the Bible did not make sense to me. I never could understand how a disconnected, fleshless anklebone, knee bone, and hipbone would somehow connect again. "And when Gabriel blows that mighty trumpet, the dead in Christ shall rise first and there is going to be a great getting up and coming together." The preacher would whoop and holler until the entire church was in a shouting frenzy. He frequently told stories about the rapture, and his word was honored above nearly everybody else's. I never wanted to be thought of as dis-

obedient by questioning anything that proceeded out of his mouth so "dry bones in the valley" it was.
I learned to enjoy attending church, mostly because my friends were there as well. After graduating high school, we went our separate ways to different universities in different cities. The most important thing to find after settling into college was a church home. Rarely had I attended a church outside of the Baptist faith. There was a little church about fifty yards from mine that sat in the bend of Nolensville Pike. You could hear them singing and playing music all the way down the street. The beating of tambourines and the loud screams of "Hallelujah" and "Praise the Lord," spilled out of the windows. Growing up, we used to call churches like this sanctified or holy rollers. Curious, my friends and I would run and press our ears against the doors of the tiny building to get a better listen. One day the church door was cracked open, and we decided to go in to find out what all the commotion was about. What we witnessed was nothing like anything we'd ever seen before. There were people dancing around in trance like states, speaking in tongues and falling out on the floor. Even the musicians had their eyes closed, playing instruments as if they were under a hypnotic spell of some sort. Excited and frightened at the same time, we bolted out of the sanctuary as fast as we could. We weren't told not to go there again, and there was nothing ill ever spoken about the little Holiness church. However, it was a tacit agreement that we stay

Lesson 18 - In the Name of Jesus

close to our church and our Baptist faith.

During my sophomore year in college, I was invited to an apostolic church. My friend Bridgette was getting married, and at the last minute the person slated to sing was not available. "Charles, I have never really heard you sing an entire song, but what I have heard is that you are a great performer. Would you be willing to sing at my wedding this Saturday?" Bridgette asked in a panic. "Today is Thursday, Bridgette. I have no idea what to sing or who I will be rehearsing with," I replied. "I will set all of that up so you can get a couple of hours of rehearsal before the wedding. Please, Charles," she begged. I said yes.
I don't remember getting much sleep at all before the rehearsal, let alone the event. Terrified, I played every worst-case scenario I could think of in my mind. What if I forget the words? What if the musician plays the song in the wrong key? What if I sing in the wrong key? I nearly talked myself out of it by the time Saturday came around. Well, what I thought would end up a disaster, turned out to be a great opportunity. Bridgette was very happy and pleased at the song selection, and the pastor of the church was so impressed that he asked if I would come back as special music guest during their Sunday morning service. One visit led to another. And though it was not a church of the same faith I grew up attending, I felt at home. After several visits, I decided that I would become a member.

New to the apostolic faith, I was eager to learn more.

One thing I noticed immediately was that many of the members demonstrated spontaneous dancing, collapsing to the floor and speaking in tongues during the service. This was very different than my Baptist upbringing where we were not taught or encouraged to act in such manner. This religious experience was not foreign behavior to me, however. Not only had I seen the likes of it while peeking through the doors of the little sanctified church down the street, but before I left for college, I had learned to speak in tongues while attending a Wednesday night Bible meeting hosted by a gentleman and his wife who I knew from my church. There was no push or demand, I allowed myself to experience this gift of the spirit, and to me it was readily accessible. My feeling about speaking in tongues was not different than what I, as a child, felt about the power of healing. What the church called the "laying on of hands" was just another way of putting what I'd always believed into action. I felt that all humans possessed the ability to release a healing virtue to another person, even if it was through a simple hug or embrace. However, the biggest difference I'd experienced in my short membership at the Apostolic church was the difference in the way people experienced baptism. In the Baptist church we were baptized in the Trinitarian manner: In the name of the Father, the Son, and the Holy Spirit. The Apostolic way was to be baptized in the name of Jesus. "Jesus only" was the faith's motto. "One way to God' was a mantra. I had no issue with this manner of being immersed under water, since Ms. Fannie taught us that it was all about Love.

With the new leadership and vision, our church was becoming a leading ministry in the city, and as word began to spread, people came from near and far to attend. Some of the most revered ministers from around the country, and the world, were called to the stage. Our annual conference would sell out days after the dates were announced.

Though my new church had changed its name after a shift in pastoral leadership, it had kept with the long-standing tradition of being a part of Pentecostal Assemblies of the World (PAW), one of the world's largest Oneness Pentecostal denominations. Many members, including myself, attended yearly conferences and convocations. However, after a few short years it was announced that our church would become independent of the giant, religious organization. I didn't realize it then, but I would soon lean how this action would create a divide within our congregation, as well as with churches of the same faith around the city. For some, removing the church from the organization was equal to blasphemy.

I quickly became an active member, entrenched in the pastor's vision and church's mission. I was responsible for guest transportation to and from the airport and would help to ensure the church was clean and secure after a busy night of events. In addition to my facility duties, I became a committed member of the church choir. It wasn't often that we had invitations to sing at other events, but every now and then we would be invited to render two songs, known in black churches as an A&B selection.

Word traveled fast in religious circles, especially in a town like Memphis that featured a church on every corner. Perhaps an entire parade of congregations had found out about our church removing itself from their coveted organization. This, in the eyes of others in the apostolic church, made us an outcast. I had learned that the side of the coin most displayed by the church seemed pleasant and uplifting, but the flip side could carry the fury of a dragon.

On one occasion, we were invited to sing at a church we had fellowship with before. A few of us arrived early to the hosting church. Since our choir was part of several groups that would be rendering selections, I asked one of the ushers if there was designated seating. "What church are you from?" she asked. After I responded, the look on her face was telling; one would have thought I had cursed her out in tongues. "Ya'll from that unsaved church," she said. "Got out of the PAW and now you done backslid." I was baffled. I didn't know how to respond. How can removing yourself from an organization cause you to backslide? That's ridiculous, I thought. "You and your choir can sit anywhere in the back—just make sure it's far away from the 'saved' folk," she snapped. I immediately felt unwelcomed. We were finally called to take the choir stand. As we prepared to sing our first song, one of the ushers paced to the stage to deliver a glass of water to one of the ministers in the pulpit. Before returning to her post, she took a quick but hard, deliberate scan of our entire choir and rolled her eyes in disgust. In exclamation, she swung her neck around so hard I thought the black doily on her head would go sailing across the room. As we sang our hearts out, the overflow crowd sat with their arms folded and their lips pressed together. They gazed at us as if they loathed our very existence. I peered out into what seemed to be a sea of judgment.

As people were exiting the sanctuary, the ushers stood at the door with well wishes. "Praise the Lord and thank you for coming. God bless you," they bid. That was until they saw us approaching the exit. I became nervous as we walked toward them, fearing they would have something rude to say. "Good riddance," one said, while another gestured her hand for us to get out. It was then that I felt the sting of hate. My stomach began to turn upside down. How can someone love God, praise Jesus, and hate at the same time? The more I thought about it, the more I realized that persecution of others whether physical, verbal, or through other actions, stems from self-persecution and the feeling of not being enough and not having enough. Their self-sufficiency lies within the validation of someone, and the attachment to something. In this cast, being part of an organization or group caused them to feel sanctified, makes them whole and "holy." Everyone they felt to be unlike them was bound to hell.

The experience at that church taught me to see people from an entirely different lens, one that accepted them as who they were and not who I wanted them to be. This spiritual charge gave me permission to embrace others without being concerned about a doctrine, but it took practice for I had been enlisted in the army of doctrinal systems for a long time. I was trying to unlearn from ways in which I had abided by the rules in the past. It's not always easy to say but, when you begin to consciously or unconsciously change who you are to suit the preferences of others, it allows the insidious thought forms that tell you that you're not enough to consume your awareness. This "not enough" consciousness initiates a cycle, which encourages you to live your life playing roles that were never meant to fit you. When left untreated or masked by a trust in man-made beliefs, this compromise can rule as imposter without you ever knowing it.

Though I was taught to stay close to my Baptist faith growing up, I don't think I was ever convinced that a religious doctrine was better than another or grounds for division of the people. In my five-year-old mind, I was aware that God was great and good to all, and that Jesus loved me and everybody else - my parent and grandparents demonstrated it so. I knew that if salvation was the connection to God, and God being Love, like Ms. Fannie Mae taught in Sunday school class, then salvation could not have been a one-time affair, but a way of living life every day. Therefore, salvation had nothing to do with belonging to a particular group. It certainly had nothing to do with hate. Hate belonged to an entirely different consciousness, thought, and action. The only way I could accept, respect, honor, and love God, Jesus, or anybody else was to first learn to love and respect myself.

"A good name is better than gold, son."

- Wilhelmina Holt

Every time I returned to college from break, my grandmother would run out on her porch, waving her hands, and admonish me to keep these words close.

Lesson 19

Finding Freedom on Christopher Street

Some things we learned easier than others. The more familiar we feel toward something, like a particular principle or way of living life, the quicker it may come to our understanding. Take freedom as an example. Freedom, at times can seem to be far from our conscious streaming. Its essence may appear to elude us for long periods of time. Then, by means of some experience or encounter, it feels as if it has come flowing back to our Soul's memory. But, in fact, freedom never left. The essential nature of freedom is everywhere we are. We are the ones who elope and run from this tower of power.

In 1996, after being in New York for two weeks, I was still learning to navigate the city by subway. I spent most of my time walking streets that I was most familiar with— those in the Theatre District. Reading the marquis at each Broadway house would amplify my excitement. The only person I knew in New York was Adrian Bailey, who was in the Broadway cast of Smokey Joe's Café. After the show, I'd often meet him at the stage door where he introduced me to other members of the production.

Sunday evenings were special because they marked the last performance. On Mondays the theatre is "dark," a term meaning that it is closed. On occasion, cast members would take trips to celebrate the end of an eight-show week and the ensuing day off. I went with them a couple of times. I would also follow along with Adrian and his friends to have a beverage and some dinner at a favorite restaurant.

One evening I decided I would let my adventurous mind lead the way. I hopped on the 42nd Street subway and headed downtown. I don't know what it was about the West 4th Street subway station that drew my attention, but I yielded to curiosity, and exited the train. Besides being one of the Manhattan's busiest subway stops, West 4th was also a destination that called to the eclectic spirit. That's somewhat hard to believe, given New York City's reputation for being a haven for people who constantly stretched the limits of ideas, style, and human behavior.

Confused about which part of the platform to exit, I made a quick turn out of the train and began walking along a slightly inclined path leading to the exit sign. I came up out the subway and landed across the street from a couple of basketball courts. It was the heat of summer, and everybody was out and about, enjoying the waning moments of daylight. The ballers were going hard at it. A crowd of people packed the perimeter of the basketball courts cheering them on. As a sports fan I thought about going over to

Lesson 19 - Finding Freedom on Christopher Street

join them, but at the last minute I opted to keep with my venturesome mind.

Not sure what direction to take, I walked toward the sun. I ended up at the entrance to another train station, located directly across the street from a park. I stood and took in the view around me for a few minutes. Clubs, bars, and little shops were everywhere. My eye, scanning across Seventh Avenue, I saw Dunkin Donuts. This was one of my favorite places to get a good donut and a cup of coffee, so I chose to regroup there before continuing my city expedition. I heard some commotion streaming from further down the street. Passing a church to the right of me, I began to feel like I had entered yet another one of the city's hidden enclaves. Trying to figure where I was, I looked at the sign on the corner: Christopher Street. I stood in amazement at the sights —what I saw was astonishing to my fresh eyes. I'd never seen people with three different colors in their hair, or women with a bull ring through their nose. I had seen men dressed as women before, but the number of male cross-dressers was countless. Men kissing and holding hands, and women doing the same was just part of the natural flow. Never had I witnessed drag queens dressed like they were going to a ball, made up from the sole of their feet to the crown of their head. Enthralled, my head was on the swivel.

Then, something in my mind caught my attention and with a huff, I halted my stride. "Whoa, Charles," I said to myself. "This is way out of your playing field. You are far beyond your land of comfort." I knew this would happen sooner or later; my religious convictions were kicking in. I began feeling the onslaught of shame and "sin." In a flash, the doctrinal sayings that had instructed my way of being for much of my life came rushing in. The self-induced autonomy and inspiration I felt while watching others carry out their lives with such liberation started to vanish into criticism. I tried cancelling the thoughts in my head, but they were coming to fast. "You know you're not supposed to hang in the company of those who don't believe like you. If they don't act like you, pray to the same God as you, and call on the name of Jesus like you were taught to do, then stay far away from them. Men who wear dresses and women who wear pants like a man are not godly. Don't let the deeds of others influence you to hell!" The condemnations continued, "Homosexuality is a sin and is sanctioned by the devil. Hold on to your salvation no matter what the cost."

    Oh, my God! My head was spinning. Once again, I was being bullied by all those thoughts of sin. I couldn't take it. I was overwhelmed by a damning conviction. In a nervous flash I ran all the way back down Christopher Street to West 4th Street, burst through the turnstiles and hopped on the first train heading uptown. Paranoid and hoping no one would see the guilt on my face, I tried to calm my heart as it raced out of control. Filled with dis-

Lesson 19 - Finding Freedom on Christopher Street

grace, I finally I made it back to Times Square and 42nd Street, but not without the biggest falling out with myself. All the way to my apartment, I prayed that I would be forgiven. I begged, "Please, God. I am so sorry."

This was not the first time I had weathered a barrage of religious assaults. Hanging out with of some of my best friends who I had played football with had caused me to conjure of thoughts of being "out of the will of God." During my first couple of years of college I would go to parties with teammates to celebrate a Saturday night victory. Feeling a heightened sense so freedom, I would dance to every song that was played. I even managed the courage of enjoying a beer - holding a cold brew in one hand and snapping to the beat of the music with the other. I was sober and on cloud nine, having the time of my life. However, the torment of my deeds awaited me. When the music stopped, that's when all hell broke loose. On the way back to my dorm room I would sink into a pit of judgment. I must say that the only way that I slipped from this noose of doom was removing myself from the very core of this mindset. I stopped going to church. I learned to decode from the religious dogma, and I started listening to the inner thoughts of what made me happy. But the voices of my religious conviction were too strong, and I eventually went back to attending church full-time and resumed my dedication to serving the Lord like the good little Christian boy my grandmother always wanted me to be.

Though far from my religious beginnings and the staunch articles of faith, I was once again faced with the nightmare of thoughts that insisted that I was "playing with a devil" that I was no match against. "Stay away from Christopher Street," I heard a voice in my mind say. But I knew I couldn't. This time, I decided I wouldn't turn back, and I'd go all the way to see what the end would be. If I was going to hell, then I wanted to go in high fashion and bust its gates wide open. My experience that Sunday on Christopher Street would not soon leave my mind. All week long I recalled what I had witnessed on Christopher Street. As much as I wished I'd never taken the turn down that street, I kept remembering the undeniable liberation I'd felt. The pictures were fixed in my head, and I could not get them out. The scent of freedom was still present in every breath, and it had permeated my entire being. Each passing day, the desire to go back grew greater. I became nervous thinking about it, but I couldn't by-pass it any longer. Something inside was pulling me to go back for another visit.

    The following Sunday I got up enough nerve to hop back on the Downtown A train. I left while the sun was still high in the sky, giving me more hours to explore. After arriving at West 4th Street, I found the same path to the exit I'd taken the week before. This time I crossed the street to watch some of the basketball game. After about thirty minutes of slam-dunks, ally oops, and some of the most incredible court tricks, I felt my nervousness kick in.

Lesson 19 - Finding Freedom on Christopher Street

As I stared down the avenue that had led me to Christopher Street, like clockwork, the thoughts of damnation began gathering in my mind. They were louder this time. But I was being pulled by something stronger. Determined, I dismissed their voices.

I began walking at a brisk pace. Feeling the palms of my hands bead with sweat, I became more courageous with each step. I walked to the Dunkin' Donuts shop, thinking that I might grab a cup of coffee. Instead, I took a deep breath and proceeded down the street where it was all happening. Once I began my tour, I relaxed my mind. I felt my body release its anxiety. I walked the length of the street at least three times, taking in all the sights and sounds. The sun was setting, but I didn't have any plans to rush back uptown. I turned back for one more stroll to the end of the street and eventually ended up at the pier.

The fun that everybody was having was contagious. Pulsing laughter and unapologetic demonstrations of love and community were what I witnessed everywhere I looked. The sun was setting, but the party seemed to just be getting started. All sorts of characters and personalities filled the streets. I walked every adjacent, parallel, and perpendicular avenue I could find. The occasion was the same in each corner of the West Village: A grand and festive coming together of people. You didn't have to dress a certain way. You didn't have to walk in a particular manner. Singles, couples, and groups were all welcomed. Each person's look was unique. The main thing that seemed to unify was the presence of freedom. People dressed like they were free and lifted their emancipated voices in full expression. Nobody was there to hurt anybody else. There was just too much fun to be had.

Not knowing how late it was, I asked a person next to me for the time. "It's going on eleven o'clock," he said. The hour was late, and past my normal bedtime. But I was wide-awake. The only thing that kept me from extending my visit was the fact that I had to be on the path of landing that Broadway show I'd moved to New York City for. I took one long exhale before calling it a night. I smiled so hard it made my temples hurt. I didn't care. I had tasted the sweet nectar of life that I had not given myself permission to experience since childhood. It was the flavor of liberation, a freedom that I knew belonged to me well before I stepped foot onto this earth.

I held a lot of things close to me growing up, and I still do. My parents remain at the top of the list of teachers; I will forever cherish my grandmother; my friends are still like family, and Lake Providence, the community in which I was raised, will always be remembered as a safe place for me to learn some of the most valuable lessons in life. I don't think any of these experiences would have been possible without my innate feeling of freedom as a child. I believed all things were kept intact by having both sides of the coin existing. However, as I matured and began carv-

Lesson 19 - Finding Freedom on Christopher Street

ing my own path of discovery, some of the things I once believed had come to the edge of my expanding mind. I realized that these lucid encounters with religious conviction were the real culprits of my shame. They were all in my mind. I realized that at the core of what I believed as a Christian was based in fear. For me to let go of the fear, I had to allow beliefs to fall away.

My visits to the West Village became frequent. Christopher Street was always a place I found to be full of beauty and community gathering. One of its many gifts was the extrication from the grip of societal and cultural beliefs. Here I could be who and what I was without judgment. Being my whole self without apology or regret is the joy of freedom, one of the greatest feelings of all.

Acknowledgements

I realize the importance and magnitude of the way my parents loved me. I feel the presence of my father and I yet hear the essence of joy through my mother's voice. I am grateful for my siblings, for my brother who, in his physical absence, continues to give me charge to share his legacy of benevolent and unconditional support of others. I will always give thanks and praise to my ancestors, those who paved the way through demonstration and wisdom, my spiritual guides, and my sacred confidants who abide with me from the invisible.

Thank you to Rickie Byars, Sheila McKeithen, Michael Beckwith, Carol Carnes, Norm Bouchard, Molly Rockey, and Carlton Pearson for your unwavering love, and for being an advocate of my work and my spiritual assignment.

To all the elders, teachers, instructors, coaches, castmates, and friends who I call family - I am forever grateful for the lessons I continue to learn from your advice, direction, and care.

To Life itself - Great Spirit, Supreme Inspiration, Universal Genius, Eternal Wisdom, and the other names that I call this divine presence. I am here by Its inspired design, and I know that my life is the life of God.

Acknowledgements

Special Praise to my friend and brother, Thanh Anderson. I salute you for all your encouraging words and for all the ways in which you demonstrated kindness. I will always love and remember you, my "good brother." Peace and Radiant Joy on your journey.

www.ingramcontent.com/pod-product-compliance
Lightning Source LLC
Chambersburg PA
CBHW021156160426
43194CB00007B/762